Jürgen Beyerer and Miro Taphanel (Eds.)

Proceedings of the 2018 Joint Workshop of Fraunhofer IOSB and Institute for Anthropomatics, Vision and Fusion Laboratory

Karlsruher Schriften zur Anthropomatik
Band 40
Herausgeber: Prof. Dr.-Ing. habil. Jürgen Beyerer

Eine Übersicht aller bisher in dieser Schriftenreihe erschienenen Bände finden Sie am Ende des Buchs.

Proceedings of the 2018 Joint Workshop of Fraunhofer IOSB and Institute for Anthropomatics, Vision and Fusion Laboratory

Edited by
Jürgen Beyerer and Miro Taphanel

KIT Scientific Publishing

Impressum

KIT Scientific Publishing

Karlsruher Institut für Technologie (KIT)
KIT Scientific Publishing
Straße am Forum 2
D-76131 Karlsruhe

KIT Scientific Publishing is a registered trademark
of Karlsruhe Institute of Technology.
Reprint using the book cover is not allowed.

www.ksp.kit.edu

Print on Demand 2019 – Gedruckt auf FSC-zertifiziertem Papier

ISSN 1863-6489
ISBN 978-3-7315-0936-3
DOI 10.5445/KSP/1000094782

Preface

In 2018, the annual joint workshop of the Fraunhofer Institute of Optronics, System Technologies and Image Exploitation (IOSB) and the Vision and Fusion Laboratory (IES) of the Institute for Anthropomatics, Karlsruhe Institute of Technology (KIT) has again been hosted by the town of Triberg-Nussbach in Germany.

For a week from July, 29 to August, 3 the PhD students of the both institutions delivered extended reports on the status of their research and participated in thorough discussions on topics ranging from computer vision and optical metrology to network security and neural networks. Most results and ideas presented at the workshop are collected in this book in the form of detailed technical reports. This volume provides a comprehensive and up-to-date overview of the research program of the IES Laboratory and the Fraunhofer IOSB.

The editors thank Lars Sommer, Julius Krause, Florian Becker, and other organizers for their efforts resulting in a pleasant and inspiring atmosphere throughout the week. We would also like to thank the doctoral students for writing and reviewing the technical reports as well as for responding to the comments and the suggestions of their colleagues.

Prof. Dr.-Ing. habil. Jürgen Beyerer
Dr.-Ing. Miro Taphanel

Contents

An Overview of Return-Path Ellipsometry

Chia-Wei Chen

Vision and Fusion Laboratory
Institute for Anthropomatics
Karlsruhe Institute of Technology (KIT), Germany
chia-wei.chen@kit.edu

Technical Report IES-2018-09

Abstract

Ellipsometry is an optical method used for characterizing materials and thin films. The principle is based on the polarization change at a sample due to the reflection or transmission at boundaries. By the measurement of the amplitude ratio Ψ and the phase difference Δ, the complex refractive index can be obtained. Ellipsometers can be used in various industries, e.g., semiconductor, chemistry, and display industry. The typical applications are quality control of film growth and defect inspection. In the configuration of return-path ellipsometry (RPE), the light beam is reflected twice from the sample. Thus, RPE has a higher sensitivity to the optical properties of samples. Some configurations of RPE have high tilt tolerance which is an important requirement for inline measurement. This report gives an introduction to the principle of ellipsometry and an overview of four different types of RPE.

1 Introduction

Ellipsometry is a widely used optical method for characterizing materials and thin films. Ellipsometers measure polarization changes at a sample in reflection or transmission configurations. This method can be applied to many different applications, for example, semiconductor, chemistry, and display industry. The advantages of ellipsometry are nondestructive measurement, high precision, and inline measurement is possible.

There are many different types of ellipsometry, for example, rotating-analyzer, phase-modulation, and return-path ellipsometry (RPE). In the configuration of RPE, the light beam reflects on the surface of the sample and returns to the same position by reflecting or retroreflecting optical elements. Compared to the conventional ellipsometry, the main feature is that RPE has a higher sensitivity to the optical properties of samples because of the double reflection from the sample. Other merits are the setup is simple, it is easy to align the system, and only one optical window is necessary for inline measurement. These merits increase the feasibility for monitoring of film growth. In this paper, we will review and compare four different types of RPE.

2 Principle of ellipsometry

Light is an electromagnetic wave which can be described by Maxwell's equations. The electric field $\boldsymbol{E}$ of a plane wave which travels along z axis can be expressed as:

$$\boldsymbol{E}(z,t) = E_0 \exp\left[\mathrm{i}\left(\omega t - Kz + \delta\right)\right],$$

where E_0 is the wave amplitude, K is the propagation number, t is the time of the wave traveling, and ω is the angular frequency. We can decompose the polarization state of the plane wave $\boldsymbol{E}$ by two fields $\boldsymbol{E}_x$ and $\boldsymbol{E}_y$ whose directions are perpendicular to each other and parallel to the z axis. Then, the full form of a plane wave can be expressed:

$$\begin{aligned}\boldsymbol{E}(z,t) &= \boldsymbol{E}_x(z,t) + \boldsymbol{E}_y(z,t)\\ &= E_{x0}\exp\left[\mathrm{i}\left(\omega t - Kz + \delta\right)\right]\boldsymbol{x} + E_{y0}\exp\left[\mathrm{i}\left(\omega t - Kz + \delta\right)\right]\boldsymbol{y},\end{aligned}$$

where $\boldsymbol{x}$ and $\boldsymbol{y}$ are unit vectors along x and y axes.

Ellipsometers can measure the complex refractive index which is defined as: $\bar{n} = n - \mathrm{i}k$, in which n is the real refractive index and k is the extinction coefficient. Fig. 2.1 shows light refraction and reflection on a substrate. In this section, only homogeneous and isotropic materials are discussed and the backside reflection is not considered. The incident light is linear polarized, of which the phase difference is 0 or 2π. After the reflection from the substrate, the reflected light becomes elliptically polarized. The Fresnel equations can be used to describe the reflection and refraction of light at boundaries. The polarization change can be defined as the ratio ρ of the amplitude reflection coefficients for p- and s-polarizations:

$$\rho = \frac{r_p}{r_s} = \tan\Psi e^{i\Delta}. \tag{2.1}$$

In Eq. (2.1), $\tan\Psi$ is the amplitude ratio for the p- and s-polarizations $(|r_p| \, / \, |r_s|)$ and Δ is the phase difference $(\delta_{rp} - \delta_{rs})$. δ_{rp} and δ_{rs} are the phase changes after reflection for the p- and s- polarizations, respectively. The angle of incidence θ_i and the refractive index of ambient $\bar{n}_i$ are usually known parameters. After the determination of Ψ and Δ by ellipsometers, the complex refractive index of the substrate can be solved by Eq. (2.2) [AB99].

$$\bar{n}_t = \bar{n}_i \tan\theta_i \sqrt{1 - \frac{4\rho}{(1+\rho)^2} \sin^2\theta_i}. \tag{2.2}$$

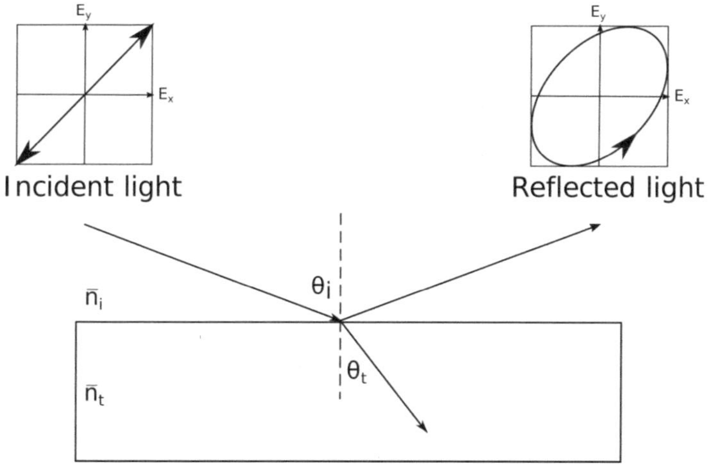

Figure 2.1: Reflection and refraction at a substrate, where $\bar{n}_i$, $\bar{n}_t$, θ_i, and θ_t are the refractive index of the ambient, and the refractive index of substrate, the incident angle, and the refraction angle, respectively.

3 Configurations of return-path ellipsometers

In this section, four existing configurations of RPE are presented. The basic principle and the main feature of these configurations will be introduced.

3.1 Plane mirror configuration

The simplest configuration of RPE was presented by O'Bryan [O'B36]. Fig. 3.1 shows a optical schematic of the plane mirror type of RPE. In his design, a Nicol prism was used as a polarizer, and a plane mirror was used to reflect the light back to the same posistion from the sample's surface. Yamaguchi and Takahashi [YT76b] modified the design of O'Bryan by replacing the Nicol prism with a Babinet-Soleil compensator and a quarter waveplate. The modified setup can measure samples at arbitrary angles without varying the incident angle. Azzam [Azz77a] used a linear polarizer and a linear retarder to replace the Nicol prism. This configuration can measure isotropic material at oblique angles of incidence and anisotropic material at a normal angle of incidence. The main feature of the plane mirror configuration is that the polarized optical components can be shared for the light source and the detector. In other words, it can reduce the number of optical elements and decrease the complexity of the system.

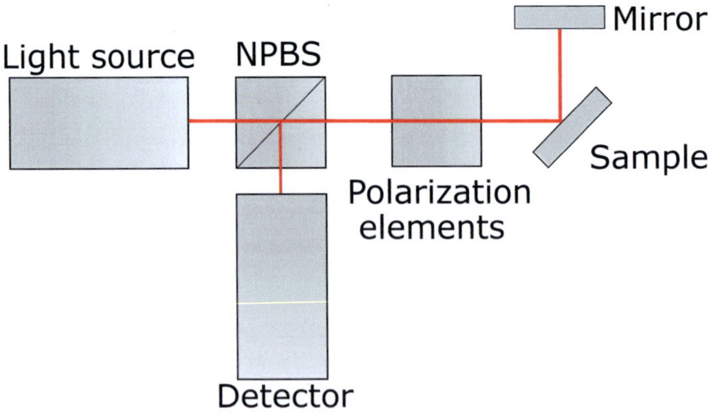

Figure 3.1: Plane mirror type of RPE: NPBS is the non-polarized beamsplitter.

3.2 Spherical mirror configuration

The plane mirror configuration, which is presented in section 3.1, is only suitable for flat surfaces because of the law of reflection. The light can be reflected back to the detector only when the plane mirror is perpendicular to the reflected ray. Slight misalignments or curved surfaces might lead to significant experimental errors. Haberland et al. [HHP+98] overcame the constraint by using a spherical mirror to replace the plane mirror. Fig. 3.2 shows the spherical mirror configuration of RPE.

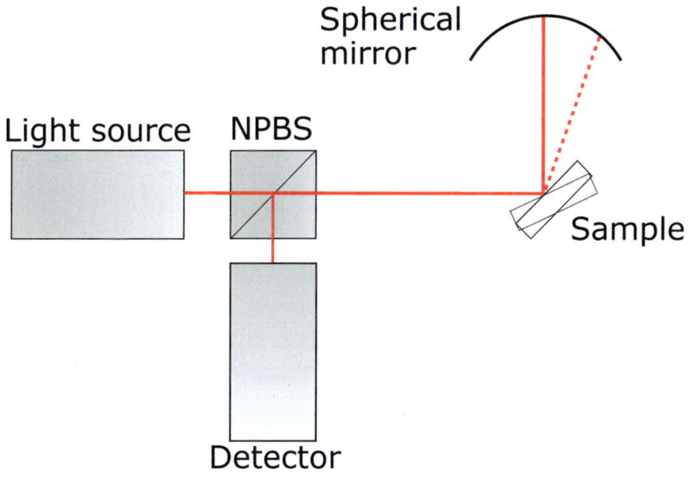

Figure 3.2: Spherical mirror type of RPE.

In geometry optics, every ray which passes the center of curvature of the spherical mirror is reflected back along the original path. Hence, the sample should be placed in the geometry center of the mirror. This configuration can effectively reduce the error from the angle deviation for sample rotation and sample wobbling, which usually occur in manufacturing process, e.g, epitaxial film growth. However, non-polarized beamsplitters usually have narrow wavelength range (e.g., 400-700 nm or 700-1100 nm) and polarization distortion [LLL16]. These disadvantages are not suitable for spectroscopic ellipsometry. Johs and He [JH11] modified the design of Haberland et al. by replacing the non-polarized beamsplitter with two right-angle prisms.The prisms have a wide wavelength range and no polarization distortion because the double reflection from the prisms cancels the change of the polarization state. The main advantage of the spherical mirror configuration of RPE is high angle tolerance while the sample is rotating or curved.

3.3 Glass hemisphere configuration

In the measurement of anisotropic material, the normal incident angle is important for the characterization of substrate birefringence. Conventional ellipsometers with two arms are difficult to measure samples at a normal incident angle due to the mechanical constraint. Fu et al. [FGS+95] proposed a method to solve this problem. The configuration is demonstrated in Fig. 3.3.

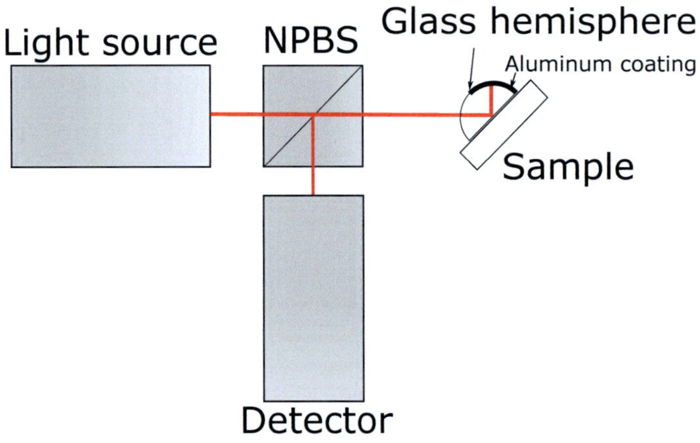

Figure 3.3: Glass hemisphere type of RPE.

A glass hemisphere is placed on the sample's surface. Half of the convex surface has aluminum coating to increase the reflectivity and the other half keeps transparent. There is no refraction in the glass hemisphere because the incident ray is perpendicular to the hemisphere all the time. Therefore, there is no polarization distortion induced by the hemisphere. The function of the hemisphere is the same as the function of the spherical mirror which was mentioned in section 3.2. The hemisphere setup, which only uses one arm, can measure samples at oblique and normal angles without obstruction and can measure samples in a transmission mode by using a transparent glass hemisphere on the top of the sample and another glass hemisphere with aluminum coating under the sample. The combined shape of two hemispheres and the sample should be a perfect sphere, which means the thickness of the sample cannot be too thick. Using glass hemispheres can reduce the size of the ellipsometer because every component is only on the same side.

3.4 Retroreflector configuration

In general, ellipsometry is a single point measurement technique and is not suitable for large-area measurement because the alignment between the sample and the system is very time-consuming. For large objects, usually only several points would be measured which would cause sampling error. Hartrumpf and Negara [HN17] developed a laser scanner with a retroreflector to overcome this limitation by using a retroreflector which is shown in Fig. 3.4. The light source is a circular polarized laser beam and a polygon mirror is used for the line scanning. The retroreflector can reflect the laser beam back to the detector with the same path and preserve the polarization state during the retroreflection [Neg14]. The advantages of the laser light source are high intensity, long coherent length, and long depth

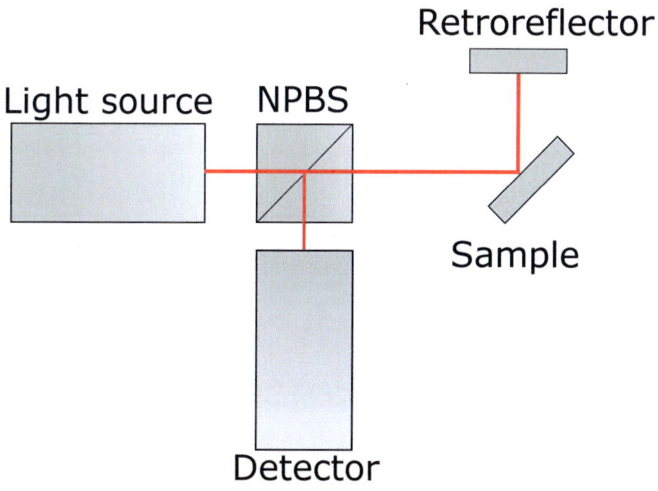

Figure 3.4: Retroreflector type of RPE.

of focus with proper focusing lenses. Because of these features and high tilt tolerance of the retroreflector, this method can be applied to curved surfaces, for example, headlight lenses, car windows, and curved displays. On the other hand, this configuration has high feasibility for inline measurement and large objects.

4 Discussion and Comparison

RPE has high sensitivity of optical properties of materials. Nevertheless, double reflection from the sample and the non-polarized beamsplitter lose a large amount of power of the light source. If a beamsplitter with a split ratio 50:50 (R:T) is used in the RPE, the power of the light source decreases to 25% because the light ray passes the beamsplitter twice. If an gold mirror ($\bar{n}_{Au} = 0.184 + 3.431i$ [JC72]) is measured at 70° with a wavelength 632.8 nm, the reflectance becomes 0.878 after double reflection from the sample. The overall power drops to 21.9%. For the low reflectivity material (e.g., N-BK7: n = 1.5151 at a wavelength 632.8 nm [Sch]), the reflectance becomes 0.03 at 70° measurement angle and the overall power drops to 0.8% . In order to compensate the power loss of the beamsplitter, the power of light source for RPE is at least four times higher than the power of the light source of conventional ellipsometers, and each surface of optical components should have anti-reflective coating to reduce the reflection loss. Another issue for the non-polarized beamsplitter is the polarization distortion. Although the beamsplitter has non-polarized effect, the polarization state of the light will change a little bit, when the light passes through the beamsplitter. Hence, the calibration for the reflection and the transmission for the beamsplitter is necessary for high-accuracy measurement. Johs and He [JH11] used two right-angle prisms to replace the beamsplitter for the elimination of the polarization distortion, but the trade-off is the positions of the first and the second reflection from the sample's surface are different. This modification of the beamsplitter is only suitable for surfaces with small angle deviation.

Table 4.1 lists the four different configurations and summarizes their advantages and disadvantages. The configurations of spherical mirror and retroreflector can overcome the angle deviation during the manufacturing process or the angle deviation of samples. The retroreflector setup has higher tilt angle tolerance compared to the spherical mirror setup because the condition of tilt immunity for the spherical mirror is only valid when the ray passes the center of the curvature of the spherical mirror. In other words, the alignment between the sample and the spherical mirror is critical. However, the retroreflector has higher polarization distortion compared to other configurations because the light beam is reflected once and refracted twice in the retroreflector. In Fresnel's equations, each reflection or refraction induces the polarization distortion. In the configuration of the glass hemisphere ball, the incident light beam is always perpendicular to the hemisphere ball for the phase conservation. This constraint increases the difficulty of the system alignment.

Table 4.1: Comparison of four different types of RPE.

	Plane mirror	Spherical mirror	Hemisphere ball	Retroreflector
Tilt tolerance	-	medium	-	high
Polarization distortion	low	very low*	low	medium
Alignment	normal	hard	hard	easy
Scanning measurement	-	-	-	possible

* The configuration of Johs and He.

5 Summary

In this report, we have introduced the basic principle of ellipsometry and four different configurations of RPE. Each configuration has its own advantages, disadvantages and suitable applications. Currently, most ellipsometers in the market are single point measurement. Measurements in these arrangements are only possible for plane surfaces or near plane surfaces. For the measurement of full-field surfaces, the measurement process is very time-consuming due to the difficulty of the alignment. In the future, we plan to use the retroreflector to design a laser scanning ellipsometer for full-field surface inspection and extend this method to curved surfaces.

Bibliography

[AB99] Rasheed Mohammed Abdel-Gawad Azzam and Nicholas Mitchell Bashara. *Ellipsometry and polarized light.* North-Holland personal library. Elsevier, Amsterdam, 4. impression, paperback ed. edition, 1999.

[Azz77a] R.M.A. Azzam. Return-path ellipsometry and a novel normal-incidence null ellipsometer (nine). *Optica Acta: International Journal of Optics*, 24(10):1039–1049, 1977.

[FGS+95] H. Fu, T. Goodman, S. Sugaya, J. K. Erwin, and M. Mansuripur. Retroreflecting ellipsometer for measuring the birefringence of optical disk substrates. *Applied Optics*, 34(1):31–39, 1995.

[HHP+98] K. Haberland, O. Hunderi, M. Pristovsek, J.-T. Zettler, and W. Richter. Ellipsometric and reflectance-anisotropy measurements on rotating samples. *Thin Solid Films*, 313-314:620–624, 1998.

[HN17] Matthias Hartrumpf and Christian Negara. *Configurable retro-reflective sensor system for the improved characterization of the properties of a sample*, 07.12.2017. WO/2017/207681.

[JC72] Peter B Johnson and R-W_ Christy. Optical constants of the noble metals. *Physical review B*, 6(12):4370, 1972.

[JH11] Blaine Johs and Ping He. Substrate wobble compensation for in situ spectroscopic ellipsometry measurements. *Journal of Vacuum Science & Technology B, Nanotechnology and Microelectronics: Materials, Processing, Measurement, and Phenomena*, 29(3):03C111, 2011.

[LLL16] Yeng-Cheng Liu, Yu-Lung Lo, and Chia-Chi Liao. Compensation of non-ideal beam splitter polarization distortion effect in michelson interferometer. *Optics Communications*, 361:153–161, 2016.

[Neg14] Christian Negara. Thickness measurement of thin films on curved surfaces with ellipsometry. In *Proceedings of the 2014 Joint Workshop of Fraunhofer IOSB and Institute for Anthropomatics, Vision and Fusion Laboratory, Karlsruher Schriften zur Anthropomatik*, volume 20, pages 49–65, 2014.

[O'B36] H. M. O'Bryan. The optical constants of several metals in vacuum*. *JOSA*, 26(3):122–127, 1936.

[Sch] Schott optical glass overview (excel table). `https://www.us.schott.com`. Accessed: 2018-12-25.

[YT76b] Tomuo Yamaguchi and Hidetoshi Takahashi. Autocollimation-type ellipsometer for monitoring film growth through a single window. *Applied optics*, 15(3):677–680, 1976.

Image-based Anomaly Detection within Crowds

Thomas Golda

Vision and Fusion Laboratory
Institute for Anthropomatics
Karlsruhe Institute of Technology (KIT), Germany
thomas.golda@kit.edu

Technical Report IES-2018-02

Abstract

Authorities and security services have to deal with more and more data collected during events and on public places. Two reasons for that are the rising number of huge events, as well as the expanding coverage with CCTV cameras of areas within cities. Even the number of ground crew teams, that are equipped with mobile cameras, rises continuously. These examples show that modern surveillance and location monitoring systems come with need of suited assistance systems, which help the associated security workers to keep track of the situations. In this report, we present a first idea how such a system using modern machine learning algorithms could look like. Furthermore, a more detailed look on two state-of-the-art methods for human pose estimation is given. These algorithms are then investigated for their performance on the target domain of crowd surveillance scenarios using a small dataset called CrowdPose.

1 Introduction

In the first part of this report, the topic of image-based anomaly detection within crowds is motivated, followed by a short characterization of the target domain.

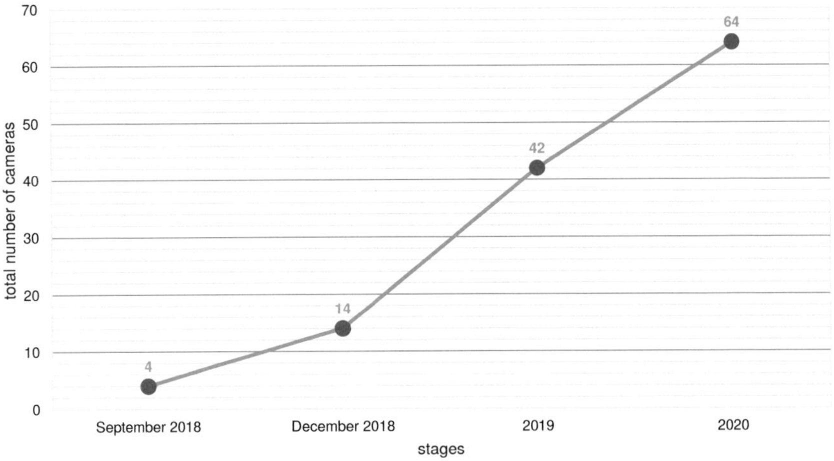

Figure 1.1: The number of cameras in the city of Mannheim will increase until 2020 up to 64 cameras and even more will follow.

1.1 Motivation

With the rising number of CCTV cameras equipped with high-resolution[1] image sensors, the task of monitoring public areas gets more and more difficult. On the one hand side, since most cameras are IP cameras, the data gathered produces large amounts of network traffic and storage utilization. On the other hand side, it is impossible for a single person to keep track of the situations within all connected cameras. As an example, the city and police of Mannheim, Germany decided to start a research project on the topic "Intelligent Video Surveillance". In cooperation with the *Fraunhofer-Institute for Optronics, System Technologies and Image Exploitation* the city center gets equipped with multiple cameras. The aim of the project in Mannheim is to do research on methods for analysing behavior of pedestrians and recognizing their activities. These methods should act as an assisting technology to help the security staff to do their job. The diagram displayed in Figure 1.1 shows how the number of cameras will develop within the

[1] 1280×720 and higher

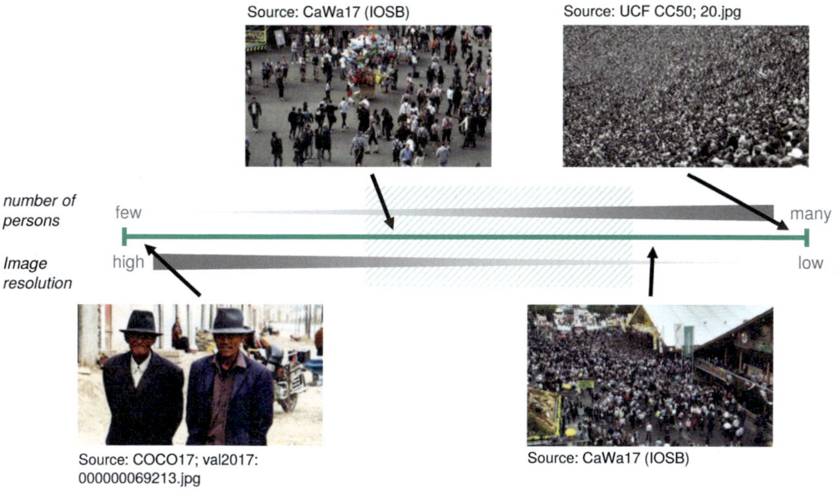

Figure 1.2: Pictures of people can range from portraits with just a single person, up to whole crowds, where the number of people shown is so high, that it is not possible anymore to detect single persons. The green hatched area shows the target domain on which this and future work will focus.

years 2018 to 2020. Another example is the Cannstatter Volksfest, an annual three-week beer festival in Stuttgart, Germany. In 2017 eleven surveillance cameras where used to monitor most of the area. The next year the number was increased by four cameras. Those examples show, that the number of cameras used at events and within cities is growing. This is a challenge not only for the security staff that has to keep an eye over all cameras, but also for the system itself, which has to cope with the large amount of data.

1.2 Characterization of the target domain

Surveillance cameras are used in various and heterogeneous environments. These are ranging from small shops, over hospitals and museums, up to large areas like the festival ground in Stuttgart where the Cannstatter Wasen takes place. Such scenarios differ in different ways, like e.g. in lighting conditions, privacy aspects and the size of the area monitored. A consequence of the last mentioned point, is the strongly varying size of single persons within the recorded video material.

Whereas a surveillance camera installed in a small shop typically records persons having a quite large size with recognizable facial features, a camera installed on a festival ground just records people with a size of only a few pixels. Figure 1.2 illustrates this situation. Pictures and video material showing people can range from single portrait pictures to images of dense crowds. Due to the strongly varying size of a single person and the different amounts of dynamic occlusions, developing a suited method is a challenging task. Therefore, it is necessary to reduce the complexity of the initial domain, which is done by concentrating on the typical views of static surveillance cameras, where some dozens of people are present.

2 Related work

Anomaly detection is an important topic in various fields, like the analysis of continuous and discrete time series [SGPE17], surveillance video streams [SCS18] and medical imaging [TCSOM+09]. All approaches have in common that they aim to develop a representation of some kind of default situation, which then is compared to the current one in order to decide whether it is an abnormal or normal situation. This is mostly done using machine learning algorithms, especially unsupervised and semi-supervised ones. The methods in the field of anomaly detection within the context of surveillance scenarios can be divided into three main categories: reconstruction models, predictive modeling, and deep generative models. [KTP18] These will be presented shortly in the following.

2.1 Reconstruction Models

This category of methods uses some intermediate representation generated from the original data. Linear and non-linear methods like principal component analysis (PCA) and Autoencoders (AE) are used to generate these representations from appearance or motion, which model the normal behavior in surveillance videos. Some representatives from this category are [XRY+15], which uses stacked de-noising Autoencoders (SDAE) to generate a representation based on input image and optical flow, [HCN+16], which uses Spatio-Temporal SDAEs on multiple stacked frames to generate a representation, and [VPN+17], which use Deep Belief Networks (DBN) for the generation of a representation. The latest publications are dominated by SDAEs, since they allow localization of anomalies compared to classical PCA and AE. [KTP18]

2.2 Predictive Models

In contrast to reconstruction models, which have the goal to learn a generative model that can reconstruct frames of a video, the goal of predictive models is to predict the current frame as a function of its predecessors. Some methods that can be counted to this category are LSTM-based methods like [WLG17] and [TBWW17], combining AEs and LSTMs, or [WS02], which use Slow Feature Analysis (SFA) that aims to extract slowly varying representations of rapidly varying high dimensional input. [KTP18]

2.3 Deep Generative Models

The last category mainly consists of Variational Autoencoders (VAE) [AC15], Generative Adversarial Networks (GAN) [DVR+18] and adversarially trained AutoEncoders (AAE), which are used for the purpose of modeling the likelihood of normal video samples in an end-to-end deep learning framework. Especially in the context of image- and video-based anomaly detection, GANs are used. The basic idea in anomaly detection is to be able to evaluate the density function of the normal vectors in the training set containing no anomalies while for the test set a negative loglikelihood score is evaluated, which serves as the final anomaly score. The score corresponds to the test sample's posterior probability of being generated from the same generative model representing the training data points. GANs provide a generative model that minimizes the distance between the training data distribution and the generative model samples without explicitly defining a parametric function, which is why it is called an implicit generative model. [KTP18]

3 Human Pose Estimation for Anomaly Detection

In Section 2 we gave an overview over existing work on anomaly detection. However, many methods like [DVR+18] and [RDFS11] use global motion context like dense optical flow for the analysis of video sequences. This is done to detect anomalies implicitly, since it is hard to tell what an anomaly looks like, beforehand. The first draft of our approach is displayed in Figure 3.1. Starting with an input image or sequence of images, the workflow consists of three major parts: the estimation of human body poses, the extraction of motion information based on (sparse) optical flow methods, and in the end a classification of the motion information. In this report, we focus on the first part shown in the schematics, namely the estimation of human body poses. The remaining parts will be part of future work.

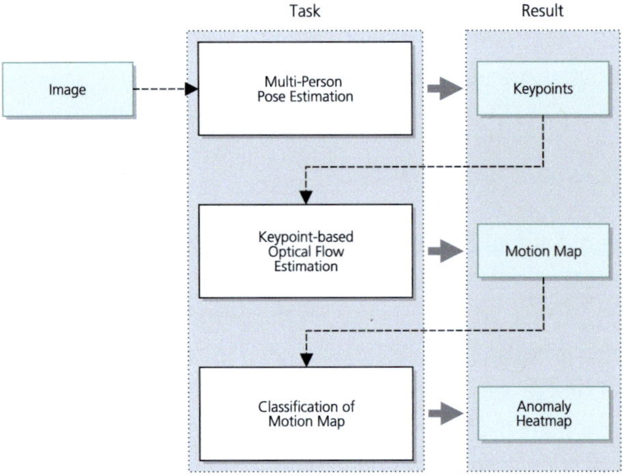

Figure 3.1: Illustration of the conceptual idea for anomaly detection based on human pose estimation. First, pose estimation is performed on the input material. The obtained key points are then tracked and classified in order to detect anomalies.

3.1 OpenPose

OpenPose [CHS^{+}18] is a framework for multi-person pose estimation. It is based on the method presented in [CSWS17], which follows a multi-stage approach. First, it generates so called *Confidence Maps* for the estimation of body key points. These maps contain information about the distribution of particular key point types within the input image. For each type of key point one Confidence Map is computed, containing estimated locations for all key points of this type within the image. Second, so called *Part Affinity Fields* (PAF) are generated. These are used for the corresponding connections between key points and contain the information, which key points might belong together, based on visible limbs or the human body. The information obtained by computing PAFs is then used in a third and last step to cluster and connect key points belonging to the same person. This is done using the Hungarian Method [KY55]. Since the algorithm's first step consists of trying to detect all key points within an image, it can be counted as a *bottom-up* method. The major benefits of bottom-down methods are their computational speed and scalability with regard to the number of persons.

3.2 AlphaPose

AlphaPose is another framework for human pose estimation. Different from OpenPose, the underlaying method belongs to the group of top-down methods. This method was presented in [FXTL17] and its main idea is to detect humans and perform single-person pose estimation on each detections, which follows the typical workflow of top-down methods. The detection-driven approach is also the main benefit of top-down methods, since they perform better for single and small persons. The main problem tackled by [FXTL17] is the avoidance of multiple pose proposals for a single person, caused by several detections of the same person. In order to achieve this, the proposed solution uses non-maximum suppression to choose the best suggested pose and iteratively removes similar pose estimates. Furthermore, as presented in [XLW+18], taking time into account improves the performance, since poses are connected over consecutive time steps. In combination with non-maximum suppression over time, this leads to more robust poses.

4 Experiments

In order to investigate how modern algorithms for image-based human pose estimation perform on data taken from the target domain, a small dataset was created. The results obtained by our experiments on this dataset and the dataset itself are presented in the following.

Figure 4.1: Examples showing patches from images taken from the CrowdPose [Dis18] dataset with corresponding annotations. The dataset consists of pictures showing different illumination situations, person sizes, number of persons and viewing angles.

4.1 CrowdPose Dataset

CrowdPose [Dis18] is a small dataset consisting of 25 different images with each image having a size of about two megapixels. In total, 833 persons were annotated over all pictures. Each image is annotated with at least six and at most 148 individuals. Figure 4.1 shows some exemplary patches taken from pictures of the CrowdPose dataset. For the annotation of the collected images we used the open source tool *sloth*.[2] We therefore developed an extension for sloth, which allowed us to annotate images with key points, automatically generated appropriate bounding boxes, person ids and activities. Despite the fact that CrowdPose is much smaller compared to other existing datasets labeled for human pose estimation like the COCO [LMB+14] and MPII [APGS14] dataset, it also differs significantly

[2] `https://github.com/cvhciKIT/sloth`

in the number of persons per image. Whereas COCO has an average number of about two persons and a maximum number of 13 persons per image, CrowdPose comes with about 33 and 148 respectively. [Ron17]

4.2 Quantitative evaluation

For the quantitative evaluation we decided to adapt the *Object Keypoint Similarity*[3] (OKS) used for the evaluation on the COCO dataset. Equation (4.1) shows the formula for the OKS.

$$\text{OKS} = \frac{\sum_i \exp(\frac{-d_i^2}{2s^2\kappa_i^2})\delta(v_i > 0)}{\sum_i \delta(v_i > 0)} \tag{4.1}$$

The d_i are the Euclidean distances between corresponding detections and ground truth points and the $v_i \in \{0, 1, 2\}$ are the visibility flags given by the dataset in order to disregard occluded keypoints from the metric. This is controlled by δ which is defined as $\min\{v_i, 2\}$. The remaining two variables are the object scale s, which is defined as the square root of the segmentation area, and a keypoint constant κ_i that has been determined by computing the standard deviation of humans by annotating multiple images redundantly. [Ron17]
Since CrowdPose does not provide any information about semantic segmentation, we could not use OKS as proposed. In order to solve this problem, we adapted OKS and replaced the segmentation area in s by the area of the resulting tightly fitted bounding boxes provided by CrowdPose. Table 4.1 shows the impact of our adapted OKS on the derived average precision ($\overline{\text{AP}}$) and average recall ($\overline{\text{AR}}$). [Dis18]

[3] http://cocodataset.org/#keypoints-eval

Table 4.1: The adapted metrics $\overline{\text{AP}}$ and $\overline{\text{AR}}$ show a similar values compared to AP and AR that were determined using the original OKS. [Dis18]

	OpenPose	**AlphaPose**
$\text{AP}_{@OKS=0.50:0.95}$	0.29912	0.41202
$\overline{\text{AP}}_{@OKS=0.50:0.95}$	0.38154	0.46619
$\text{AR}_{@OKS=0.50:0.95}$	0.32849	0.42581
$\overline{\text{AR}}_{@OKS=0.50:0.95}$	0.40806	0.47581

Since the $\overline{\text{AP}}$ and $\overline{\text{AR}}$ are in competing range to AP and AR, we were encouraged to use the adapted OKS for our experiments.
Table 4.2 shows evaluation results on CrowdPose for OpenPose and AlphaPose. AlphaPose beats OpenPose in all experiments achieving up to 8.3 times higher performance. It is conspicuous, that all obtained results are much lower compared to the evaluation results on COCO dataset displayed in Table 4.1.

Table 4.2: The table shows $\overline{\text{AP}}$ / $\overline{\text{AR}}$ for AlphaPose and OpenPose on CrowdPose dataset. Both methods were evaluated on the whole CrowdPose dataset, as well as on both its subsets. AlphaPose outperforms OpenPose in all experiments. [Dis18]

	Combined	**Cannstatter Wasen**	**IOSB**
AlphaPose	0.00349 / 0.01297	0.00006 / 0.00359	0.01249 / 0.06103
OpenPose	0.00088 / 0.00324	0.00003 / 0.00043	0.00231 / 0.01765

The main reason for this can be found in the evaluation process itself. As presented earlier, OKS uses some key point constants, which were obtained using annotated images from COCO dataset. If we compare the appearance of CrowdPose images and those from COCO, we can see that those from CrowdPose differ significantly to those from the latter. It seems that the determined key point constants cannot be used directly for the evaluation on CrowdPose. Especially the adaption using the scale s might have a strong influence on the sensitivity of the metric to the size of a single person and hence the actual key point locations. For all experiments, the methods were used without any changes and without further fine-tuning on the target domain.

Figure 4.2: Exemplary result generated with AlphaPose. On the the first glance, the left side shows promising results. The right part shows a central patch taken from the left image. The red arrow indicates a wrong connection between key points of different persons, which is just one of multiple wrong poses within the patch.

4.3 Qualitative evaluation

Despite the strong discrepancy of the quantitative evaluation results between the evaluation on COCO and CrowdPose presented in Section 4.2, the qualitative results show promising results. Figure 4.2 shows an evaluation example generated using AlphaPose. At first glance, the result looks good. However, when we take a more detailed look on this example, we can see some apparent failures. The most salient one is indicated by the red arrow: obviously, a wrong connection has been predicted between two persons. Furthermore, especially when two or more persons overlap, often body skeletons are predicted over multiple persons. Two examples within the patch are the two guys on the right hand side, and the two girls in the bottom right part. Nonetheless, the evaluation shows that human pose estimation is suited for the application on the target domain. In order to improve the results, the state-of-the-art methods have to be slightly adapted in order to be more robust against overlapping persons and obviously wrong inter-connections between unrelated persons. These problems will be tackled in future work.

5 Summary and Future Work

In this report, we presented an overview over existing methods for image-based anomaly detection within crowded scenarios. Furthermore, we introduced the field of human pose estimation and evaluated two state-of-the-art algorithms for their performance on the CrowdPose dataset, which was created to investigate the methods apart from typical application scenarios. The two algorithms, OpenPose [CHS+18] and AlphaPose [FXTL17], representing the two main approaches for human pose estimation performed similarly well. The broadly used metric OKS used by the COCO keypoint challenge [LMB+14], reports quite bad results on the own dataset. However, the qualitative evaluation showed promising results. In future work we will mainly concentrate on three different essential aspects that came up during our first experiments: the adaption of existing methods for human pose estimation to the target domain of crowded scenarios, a mathematical definition of anomalies in crowded scenarios and the application of human pose estimation algorithms for anomaly detection.

Bibliography

[AC15] Jinwon An and Sungzoon Cho. Variational autoencoder based anomaly detection using reconstruction probability. 2015.

[APGS14] Mykhaylo Andriluka, Leonid Pishchulin, Peter Gehler, and Bernt Schiele. 2d Human Pose Estimation: New Benchmark and State of the Art Analysis. In *IEEE Conference on Computer Vision and Pattern Recognition (CVPR)*, June 2014.

[CHS+18] Zhe Cao, Gines Hidalgo, Tomas Simon, Shih-En Wei, and Yaser Sheikh. OpenPose: realtime multi-person 2D pose estimation using Part Affinity Fields. In *arXiv preprint arXiv:1812.08008*, 2018.

[CSWS17] Zhe Cao, Tomas Simon, Shih-En Wei, and Yaser Sheikh. Realtime multi-person 2d pose estimation using part affinity fields. In *CVPR*, 2017.

[Dis18] Thomas Dissert. *Posenerkennung von Personen innerhalb von Menschenmengen*. KIT, Karlsruhe, 2018.

[DVR+18] Lucas Deecke, Robert Vandermeulen, Lukas Ruff, Stephan Mandt, and Marius Kloft. Anomaly detection with generative adversarial networks, 2018.

[FXTL17] Hao-Shu Fang, Shuqin Xie, Yu-Wing Tai, and Cewu Lu. RMPE: Regional multi-person pose estimation. In *ICCV*, 2017.

[HCN+16] Mahmudul Hasan, Jonghyun Choi, Jan Neumann, Amit K. Roy-Chowdhury, and Larry S. Davis. Learning temporal regularity in video sequences. *2016 IEEE Conference on Computer Vision and Pattern Recognition (CVPR)*, pages 733–742, 2016.

[KTP18] B. Ravi Kiran, Dilip Mathew Thomas, and Ranjith Parakkal. An overview of deep learning based methods for unsupervised and semi-supervised anomaly detection in videos. *Journal of Imaging*, 4(2), 2018.

[KY55] H. W. Kuhn and Bryn Yaw. The hungarian method for the assignment problem. *Naval Res. Logist. Quart*, pages 83–97, 1955.

[LMB+14] Tsung-Yi Lin, Michael Maire, Serge J. Belongie, Lubomir D. Bourdev, Ross B. Girshick, James Hays, Pietro Perona, Deva Ramanan, Piotr Dollár, and C. Lawrence Zitnick. Microsoft COCO: common objects in context. *CoRR*, abs/1405.0312, 2014.

[RDFS11] D. Ryan, S. Denman, C. Fookes, and S. Sridharan. Textures of optical flow for real-time anomaly detection in crowds. In *2011 8th IEEE International Conference on Advanced Video and Signal Based Surveillance (AVSS)*, pages 230–235, Aug 2011.

[Ron17] Matteo Ruggero Ronchi. COCO 2017 Keypoints Challenge, October 2017.

[SCS18] W. Sultani, C. Chen, and M. Shah. Real-world anomaly detection in surveillance videos. In *2018 IEEE/CVF Conference on Computer Vision and Pattern Recognition*, pages 6479–6488, June 2018.

[SGPE17] Dominique T. Shipmon, Jason M. Gurevitch, Paolo M. Piselli, and Stephen T. Edwards. Time series anomaly detection; detection of anomalous drops with limited features and sparse examples in noisy highly periodic data. *CoRR*, abs/1708.03665, 2017.

[TBWW17] Eleni Tsironi, Pablo Barros, Cornelius Weber, and Stefan Wermter. An analysis of convolutional long short-term memory recurrent neural networks for gesture recognition. *Neurocomput.*, 268(C):76–86, December 2017.

[TCSOM+09] Alberto Taboada-Crispi, Hichem Sahli, Maykel Orozco Monteagudo, Denis Hernández-Pacheco, and Alexander Falcon. *Anomaly Detection in Medical Image Analysis*, pages 426–446. 01 2009.

[VPN+17] Hung Vu, Dinh Q. Phung, Tu Dinh Nguyen, Anthony Trevors, and Svetha Venkatesh. Energy-based models for video anomaly detection. *CoRR*, abs/1708.05211, 2017.

[WLG17] W. Liu W. Luo and S. Gao. Remembering history with convolutional lstm for anomaly detection. In *2017 IEEE International Conference on Multimedia and Expo (ICME)*, 2017.

[WS02] Laurenz Wiskott and Terrence J. Sejnowski. Slow feature analysis: Unsupervised learning of invariances. *Neural Comput.*, 14(4):715–770, April 2002.

[XLW+18] Yuliang Xiu, Jiefeng Li, Haoyu Wang, Yinghong Fang, and Cewu Lu. Pose Flow: Efficient online pose tracking. In *BMVC*, 2018.

[XRY+15] Dan Xu, Elisa Ricci, Yan Yan, Jingkuan Song, and Nicu Sebe. Learning deep representations of appearance and motion for anomalous event detection. *CoRR*, abs/1510.01553, 2015.

Application of diffractive optical elements in confocal microscopy

Zheng Li

Vision and Fusion Laboratory
Institute for Anthropomatics
Karlsruhe Institute of Technology (KIT), Germany
zheng.li@kit.edu

Technical Report IES-2018-03

Abstract

In traditional confocal microscopy, there is a tradeoff between the spatial resolution and the field of view due to the limitations of the objective lenses. To solve this problem, diffractive optical elements (DOEs) are used to generate illumination spots with high NA in a large area simultaneously. However, such DOEs in current research are only used as illuminators. In this work, the idea of superposition is utilized in DOEs to have flexible functionality and replace high-NA objectives for confocal measurement. To design the DOEs, different numerical simulation methods for light propagation are investigated and compared. Rayleigh-Sommerfeld integral is chosen to simulate the DOEs to get accurate results. Two kinds of DOEs are designed and simulated for 3D confocal surface measurements.

1 Introduction

Confocal microscopy has long become the golden standard in life sciences and other fields [VBR+15]. In a simple single-spot laser scanning confocal microscope, a very focused spot is produced by an objective to illuminate a tiny part of the object. The bright spot on the object is again imaged by the objective onto the image sensor. A pinhole is used to block out-of-focus light scattered by the object to have a sharper image of the spot on the object. In this way, much better

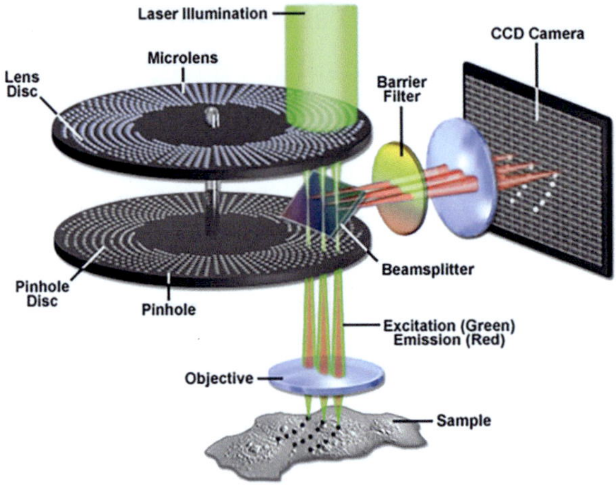

Figure 1.1: Optical configuration of a spinning disk microscope [DSS$^+$09].

axial resolution than wide-field microscopy can be achieved and 3D images of the object can be obtained through layer-by-layer scanning. Furthermore, a multi-spot array can be used to increase the scanning speed. For example, Fig. 1.1 shows a Nipkow spinning disk which produces multiple spots to faster scan the sample.

One of the key components in a confocal microscope is the objective. The resolution of the microscope is directly related to the produced spot size, and the spot size is determined by the numerical aperture of the objective. The numerical aperture is defined as in Eq. (1.1), where n is the refractive index of the medium in which the objective works and θ is the half angle of the light cone which the objective can collect.

$$\mathrm{NA} = n \sin\theta \tag{1.1}$$

High-NA objectives provide better resolution. However, high-NA objectives with large diameters, e.g. lithography lenses, are very difficult and expensive to design and produce, which makes them impractical for microscopic applications [Zhe16]. Objectives need to get closer to the sample with the increase of NA. This leads to a limited field of view, which means only a small portion of the sample can be scanned at once. Besides, due to the complex structures of high-NA lenses, they are also very expensive.

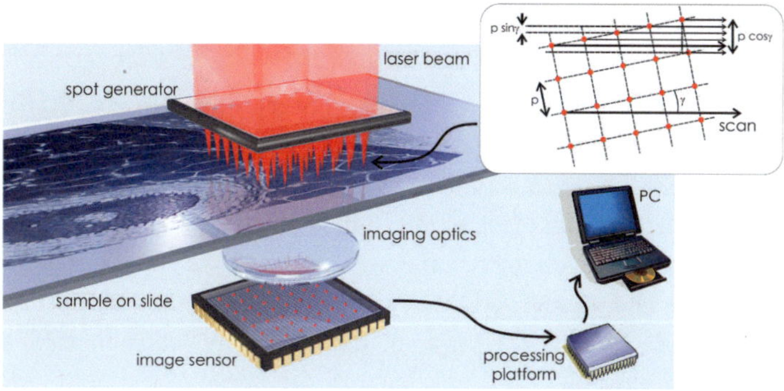

Figure 1.2: Optical configuration of a multi-spot scanning microscope using a DOE [HVS12].

In order to solve these problems, using DOEs as array illuminators has been proposed to scan large-area samples with comparable resolution to the standard confocal microscopy [HVS12][LSB12][LB14].

Fig. 1.2 shows the principle of a multi-spot scanning microscope based on a DOE illuminator. In this case, the DOE acts as an array of Fresnel lenses with overlapping apertures. It focuses plane wave into tiny illumination spots. A complete image of the sample is obtained by scanning it with the spot array. The array is placed at an angle to the scanning direction which allows one-axis scanning for a 2D plane.

However, such DOEs are not suitable for measuring 3D surfaces of opaque samples, because the spots cannot be imaged from the same side through the DOEs. So the imaging systems must be placed on the opposite sides of the DOEs and only transparent or semi-transparent samples can be measured. In order to avoid this limitation, we propose new kinds of DOEs which utilize superposition of different field distributions to allow more flexible functionality.

In the following sections, the simulation and the design methods for the DOEs are described. Two design concepts of DOEs are proposed which enable 3D surface measurements for opaque samples. The functionality and limitation of the DOEs are discussed based on the simulation results.

2 Diffraction simulation methods

To design such DOEs, one follows the procedures shown in Fig. 2.1 [HVS12]. First, a target field distribution is created, which is a spot array in this case. Then it propagates back through a certain working distance by simulation and the field distribution on the working plane of the DOE is obtained. In this case, the DOE is simply a piece of glass with micro structures etched on the surface. The structures are micro peaks and valleys, and they can control the phase of light to form a designed pattern. So only the phase of the field distribution is used, because a DOE made of pure glass can only control the phase of the field. Moreover, for manufacturing convenience, the phase is binarized because etching a binary profile on the glass is the easiest. The binarized phase then represents the micro peaks and valleys on the glass surface of the DOE. Finally, the binarized phase propagates again through the designed working distance by simulation to examine the produced spot array.

To make a DOE which can produce the same pattern as designed, the key in the above-mentioned procedures is to accurately calculate the field distribution after it propagates a certain distance. This is also the central problem for a diffraction simulation as Fig. 2.2 shows, where we want to calculate the field distribution $u(x, y, z)$ after the initial field at $z = 0$ propagates a certain distance through a medium with the refractive index n. Traditional geometrical optics methods like ray tracing are not able to simulate the diffraction phenomenon.

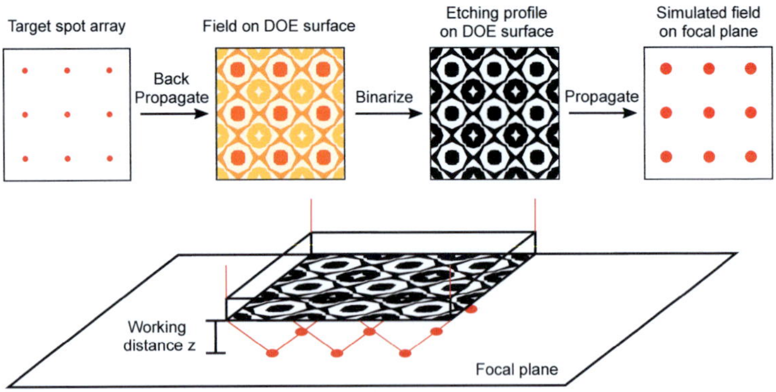

Figure 2.1: Design procedures of the DOE [HVS12]. The patterns are only for demonstration purpose and they are not generated by a real simulation.

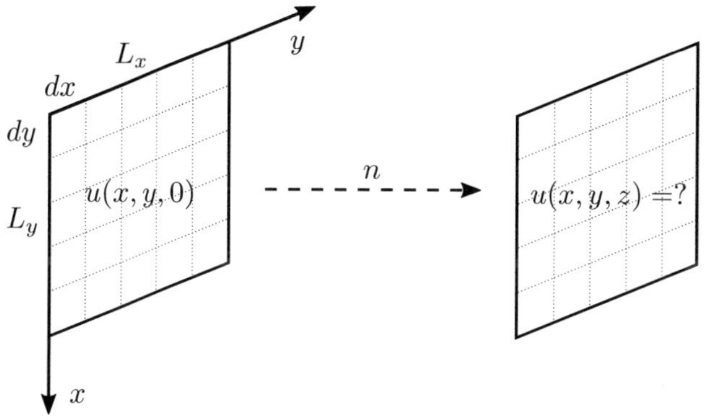

Figure 2.2: Calculating the field distribution after propagating a certain distance.

Meanwhile, full-wave solvers like FDTD or FEM can provide most accurate results by spatially discretizing Maxwell's equations in the computational domain. However, due to the huge size of the discretized grid for our 3D simulation scale in the millimeter range and the wavelength in the near-infrared spectrum, these methods would take months or years for a single run on normal servers even with GPU acceleration, which makes it inefficient for iterative design and optimization. So the classical diffraction theory in Fourier optics which uses scalar approximation for the Maxwell's equations is the suitable choice and now becomes the cornerstone for analysis of diffraction in wave optics [Voe11].

Generally, the propagation of light, which is identified as electromagnetic wave [Max65], is governed by Maxwell's equations:

$$\begin{cases} \dfrac{\partial \mathbf{D}}{\partial t} &= \nabla \times \mathbf{H}, \\ \dfrac{\partial \mathbf{B}}{\partial t} &= -\nabla \times \mathbf{E}, \\ \nabla \cdot \mathbf{B} &= 0, \\ \nabla \cdot \mathbf{D} &= 0. \end{cases}$$

With time-harmonic field and scalar approximation, Maxwell's equations are simplified into scalar Helmholtz's Equation [Goo05][KH14]:

$$\Delta u(\mathbf{r}, \omega) + k^{\mathbf{2}} u(\mathbf{r}, \omega) = \mathbf{0}, \tag{2.1}$$

where u is the scalar field of light which replaces $\mathbf{E}$ and $\mathbf{H}$ since they both satisfy the above equation, $\mathbf{r} = (x, y, z)$ is the coordinate, ω is the angular frequency of the light which we drop afterwards for simplicity since the frequency dependency is implicitly assumed, $k = 2\pi n/\lambda$ is the wave number where n is the refractive index of the medium and λ is the wavelength. The accuracy of the scalar approximation in diffraction is discussed in [Sil62][Lin72][BGG98]. They have shown that the scalar theory can yield sufficiently accurate results when the diffracting aperture size and observation distance from the aperture are both large compared to the wavelength, which is applicable in our case with the aperture size and the working distance in millimeter range.

Under the scalar approximation, there are two exact solutions for the scalar Helmholtz Equation (2.1) with the boundary condition on an opaque screen with finite apertures:

$$u(x, y, 0) = u_0(x, y), \tag{2.2a}$$

and the Sommerfeld radiation condition:

$$\lim_{|\mathbf{r}| \to \infty} |\mathbf{r}| \left(\frac{\partial u(\mathbf{r})}{\partial |\mathbf{r}|} - iku(\mathbf{r}) \right) = \mathbf{0}, \tag{2.2b}$$

which implies that the wave should decay when propagating to the infinity and no wave should be radiated back from the infinity.

With the boundary condition (2.2a) and (2.2b), one solution is known as the Rayleigh-Sommerfeld integral [Som96][Som04]:

$$u(\mathbf{r}) = \iint_{\Sigma} u_o(\mathbf{r}') \frac{e^{-ik|\mathbf{r}-\mathbf{r}'|} z}{|\mathbf{r} - \mathbf{r}'|^2} dx' dy', \tag{2.3}$$

where Σ denotes the surface on the boundary, i.e. the aperture plane and the semi-infinite sphere behind it, $\mathbf{r}' = (x', y', z')$ is the coordinate on Σ.

The other solution is the angular spectrum method [BRS50] as the following equation shows, which is also the simulation method used in [HVS12]:

$$u(\mathbf{r}) = \iint_{-\infty}^{\infty} U_o(\alpha, \beta) e^{-i\gamma(\alpha,\beta) z} e^{-i(\alpha x + \beta y)} d\alpha d\beta, \tag{2.4}$$

where $U_0(\alpha, \beta) = \left(\frac{1}{2\pi}\right)^2 \iint_{-\infty}^{\infty} u_o(x, y) e^{i(\alpha x + \beta y)} d\alpha d\beta$

is the Fourier transform of the initial field distribution at $z = 0$. α, β and $\gamma(\alpha, \beta)$ are called spatial frequencies which satisfy the relation $k^2 = \alpha^2 + \beta^2 + \gamma^2$. Equ. (2.4) implies that $u(\mathbf{r}) = u(x, y, z)$, which is the field distribution after $u_0(x, y) = u(x, y, 0)$ propagating a distance z, equals to the inverse Fourier transform of the product of $U_0(\alpha, \beta)$ and $e^{-i\gamma(\alpha,\beta)z}$.

Both solutions can solve the distribution of a field after propagating a defined distance as Fig. 2.2 shows. The angular spectrum method is in spatial frequency domain and the Rayleigh-Sommerfeld integral in real spatial domain. Analytically, they are equivalent and will provide the same simulation results. However, numerically they show different behaviour and are therefore suitable for solving different problems.

The reason is due to the sampling of these two integrals. Knowing the initial field distribution $u_0(x, y)$, we want to calculate the new field $u(x, y, z)$. Because analytic solutions of them are not known, they are calculated numerically. The first step is to discretize the initial field $u_0(x, y)$ as Fig. 2.2 shows.

For the Rayleigh-Sommerfeld integral in Eq. (2.3), the sampling is straightforward. If the initial field u_0 is discretized into smaller pieces, the sampling interval dx' and dy' also becomes smaller and the product inside the integral has a higher sampling rate. Generally, when the computational pixel size is smaller than a half of the wavelength, the integral is sufficiently well sampled [SW06].

However, for the angular spectrum method, the sampling is different due to the Fourier transform. As Eq. (2.4) shows, the angular spectrum method is the inverse Fourier transform of the product of $U_0(\alpha, \beta)$ and an oscillating phase $e^{-i\gamma(\alpha,\beta)z}$. This product has to be sampled sufficiently. On the one hand, $U_0(\alpha, \beta)$ is the Fourier transform of $u_0(x, y)$. So dx and dy need to be small enough to avoid aliasing in the frequency domain. On the other hand, $e^{-i\gamma(\alpha,\beta)z}$ will be sufficiently sampled when the phase of the oscillating term varies by less than π in each sampling step. This means that the sampling interval $d\alpha$ and $d\beta$ also has to be small enough to have a small variation step of $\gamma(\alpha, \beta)$. The size of $d\alpha$ and $d\beta$ is proportional to $1/L_x$ and $1/L_y$ in Fig. 2.2. This requires a computational window size which should be large enough to resolve $\gamma(\alpha, \beta)$. Besides, the propagation distance z should also be short enough.

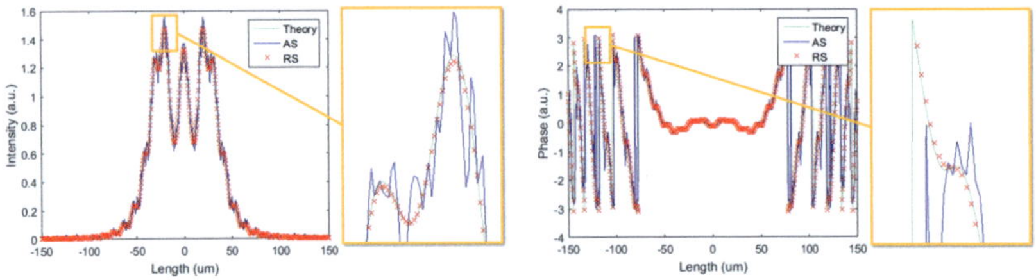

(a) Intensity of the fields after the slit. (b) Phase of the fields after the slit.

Figure 2.3: Simulation of the field distribution after a 1D slit by different methods.

These restrictions require a large computational window and small pixels simultaneously in certain cases. In our simulation scale, we have found that the angular spectrum method needs large zero padding which will lead to a large number of total computational pixels and a longer runtime.

Moreover, the angular spectrum method will have an implicit assumption of a periodic boundary condition due to the property of the discrete Fourier transform which needs to be treated carefully. The Rayleigh-Sommerfeld integral assumes zero boundary conditions which is easier to handle.

Fig. 2.3 shows the field distribution of a $100\,\mu\text{m}$ 1D slit after propagating a distance of $1\,\text{mm}$, which is a 2D simulation. The wavelength is $1\,\mu\text{m}$. The total simulation length is $300\,\mu\text{m}$. In such a simulation scale, we can see that the Rayleigh-Sommerfeld integral fits better with the theoretical result, while the angular spectrum method shows more oscillations and deviations. The detailed numerical implementation for the Rayleigh-Sommerfeld integral can be found in [SW06], and that for the angular spectrum method is almost identical to the common Fresnel diffraction implementation in [Voe11].

By the Rayleigh-Sommerfeld integral, we made a simulation with the computational window size $L_x = L_y = 2.4\,\text{mm}$, the pixel size $dx = dy = 0.4\,\mu\text{m}$ and the propagation distance $z = 1\,\text{mm}$. The runtime for a single propagation is around $17\,\text{s}$, which is sufficiently short for iterative design and optimization. Thus the Rayleigh-Sommerfeld integral is chosen as the simulation method in this work. All the DOE design in the following chapter is simulated by it.

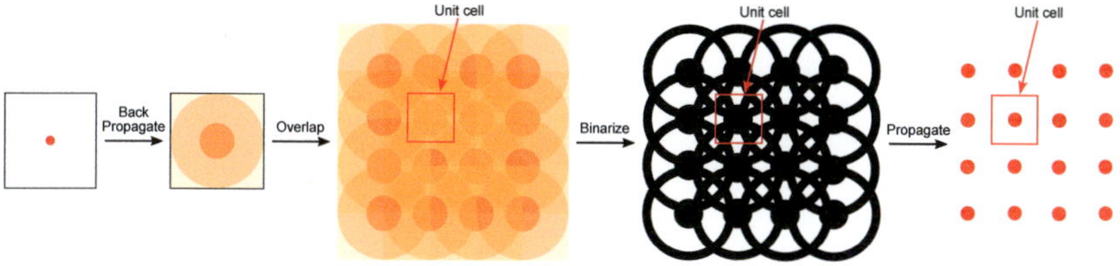

Figure 3.1: The DOE generates spot array with overlapping apertures. The patterns are only for demonstration purpose and they are not generated by a real simulation.

3 DOE Design for surface measurements

3.1 Overlapping apertures and multi-functional DOEs

To use the DOEs to replace high-NA objectives for fast scanning with high resolution, they need to be able to produce dense spot arrays with high-NA. This is achieved by the concept of overlapping apertures. As shown in Fig. 2.1, the spot array is produced by the DOE which is composed of periodic unit cells. However, a single spot in the array is not only produced by the unit cell right above it. It also receives contributions from all unit cells around the spot [HVS12]. This is equivalently explained by the design procedures in Fig. 3.1. The spot propagates back and forms a spherical-wave-like field distribution. In order to construct a spot array, this field is duplicated and overlapped with a certain pitch. Then the overlapping field is binarized and propagates back to verify the spot array which will be actually produced. In this case, the spot is not solely produced by the small unit cell above it, but it will be produced by the original spherical-wave-like field which is already overlapped with the adjacent ones. Thus, the NA of the spot is not limited by the pitch anymore. A dense spot array with high NA can be generated in this way.

However, as described in Section 1, such DOEs are not capable of measuring opaque objects. To improve the measurement capability of such DOEs in the current research, the key idea is the superposition of different field distributions. By simply adding different fields generated from different target light distributions, all the target patterns can be generated with one single DOE [DZXL03]. Such kind of DOEs is known as the multi-functional DOEs.

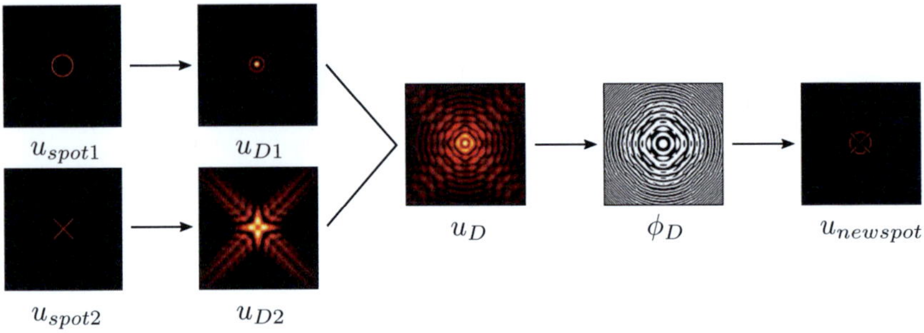

Figure 3.2: Design procedures for multi-functional DOEs.

For example, if one DOE can generate a circle and another one can generate a cross, the combined DOE of the previous two DOEs can generate a circle and a cross at the same time. Fig. 3.2 demonstrates the design procedures and simulation results for this DOE. u_{spot1} and u_{spot2} are the field distributions of a circle and a cross. u_{D1} and u_{D2} are the field distributions on the the working plane after u_{spot1} and u_{spot2} propagate back a certain working distance respectively. Then they are simply added together with a weight factor W and form a new field distribution:

$$u_D(x, y) = u_{D1}(x, y) + W u_{D2}(x, y). \tag{3.1}$$

Afterwards, the phase of u_D is extracted and binarized into ϕ_D with a binarization factor B [HVS12]:

$$\phi_D(x, y) = \mod\left(\left\lfloor \frac{\arg[u_D(x, y)] + B}{\pi} \right\rfloor, 2\right)\pi. \tag{3.2}$$

Finally, with plane-wave illumination, the binary DOE forms a field distribution e^{ϕ_D} and it propagates to the focal plane to show the actual pattern $u_{newspot}$, which in this case is the superposition of a circle and a cross. With this method, a single piece of a DOE can have a more flexible functionality. In the following sections, two DOE designs will be introduced to overcome the shortcomings of the previous DOEs in Fig. 2.1 for confocal microscopy. These designs utilize the idea of superposition to realize see-through and direct-imaging functions and are both able to measure opaque surfaces.

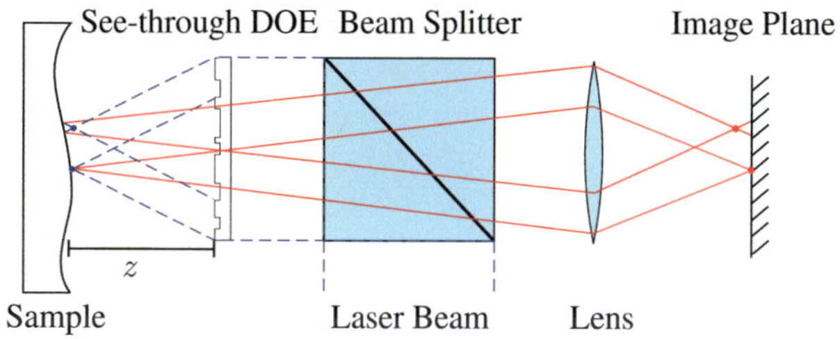

Figure 3.3: See-through configuration of a DOE-based confocal surface measurement system.

3.2 See-through DOE design

In order to illuminate and image the sample on the same side for confocal surface measurements, the spots need be able to be seen through the DOE without too much disturbance.

Fig. 3.3 shows a DOE-based multi-spot scanning confocal microscope for surface measurements. The dashed blue lines represent the illumination light and the solid red lines represent the light refelcted from the sample. The DOE generates high-NA spots which are imaged by a low-NA objective lens. In this way, although the low-NA lens will produce large spots on the image plane, the lateral resolution is still governed by the high-NA illumination spots, which is similar to the principle of super-resolution microscopy like STED or PALM [HW94][BPS$^+$06]. Meanwhile, a low-NA lens can offer a large field of view. Thus high resolution and large-area scanning can be achieved at the same time.

Fig. 3.4 shows a section of the simulated image for a 21×21 spot array with a pitch of $20\,\mu\text{m}$, which is generated by a DOE with an NA of 0.7 and imaged by a lens with an NA of 0.2. The wavelength for the simulation is $785\,\text{nm}$ The DOE multi-spot illuminator is designed in the similarly to the procedures described in [HVS12].

It is obvious that the spots are severely disturbed when they are imaged through the DOE. We are going to define an intensity contrast factor (ICF). The definition of it is going to be the ratio between the intensity of the central pixel on the image and the average intensity of the following unit cell:

$$\text{ICF} = \frac{I_{center}}{I_{mean}}.$$

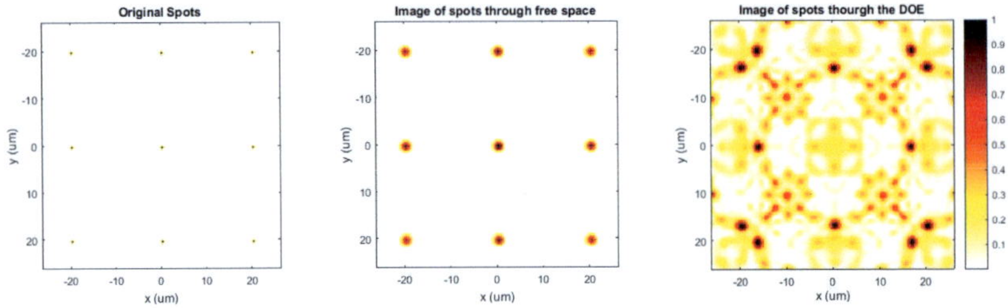

(a) 3×3 grid section in a 21×21 spot array.

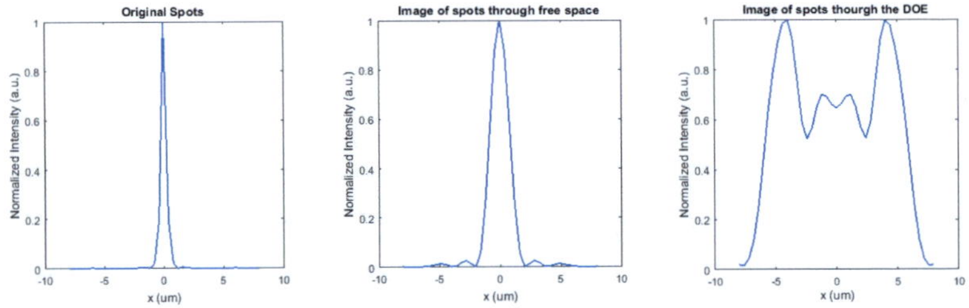

(b) Cross section of the intensity profile near central spot at $y = 0$.

Figure 3.4: Simulation of spots generated and imaged through a pure DOE illuminator.

In the ideal case, when a perfect spot array is imaged by such a configuration, the ideal ICF $= 116.38$. For the simulation in Fig. 3.4, we get the ICF $= 1.97$. As clearly shown in the very noisy picture, such DOEs are not capable for surface measurements when illumination and imaging systems are on the same side of the sample.

To reduce the disturbance added by the DOE itself, a plane-wave component is added to the original DOE. This is simply done as described in Section 3.1 by putting $u_{D2}(x, y) = 1$ as plane wave into Eq. (3.1):

$$u_D(x, y) = u_{D1}(x, y) + W,$$

where u_{D1} is the field distribution to produce a spot array like Fig. 2.1. In this way, the new DOE can not only generate a spot array, but also act as a transparent piece of glass which lets the low-NA objective to image the spots through it without too much disturbance. The simulation results of such a DOE is shown in Fig. 3.5 for a spot array with the same wavelength, spot number, pitch and NA as Fig. 3.4. The DOE is optimized iteratively with the working distance $z = 1.095\,\mathrm{mm}$, the weight

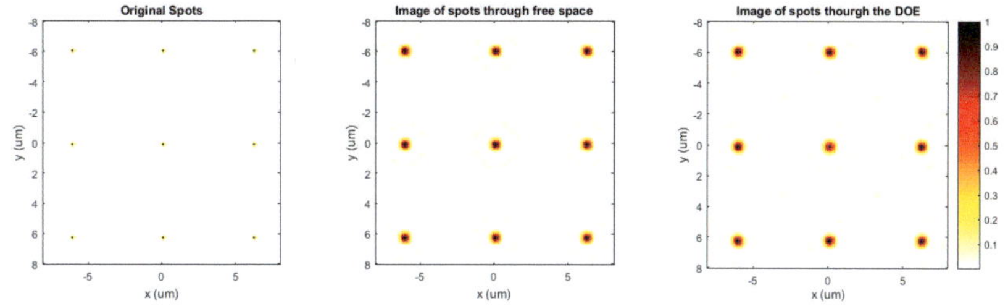

(a) 3×3 grid section in a 21×21 spot array.

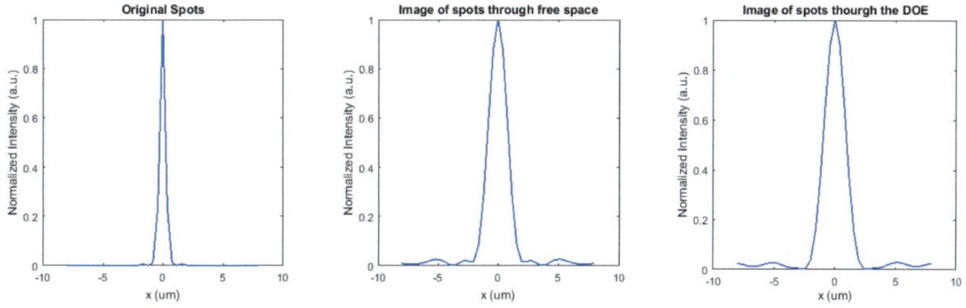

(b) Cross section of the intensity profile near central spot at $y = 0$.

Figure 3.5: Simulation of spots generated and imaged through a see-through DOE with a plane-wave component.

factor $W = 18$ and the binarization factor $B = 0.49\pi$ in Eq. (3.2) to achieve the highest intensities in the spot centers. Compared to the image simulation of the previous DOE, it is obvious that the spots are much less disturbed and can be clearly imaged by the low-NA objective with a highly improved ICF $= 48.25$.

Such DOEs can realize the concept of combining high-NA illumination and low-NA imaging for confocal surface measurements, which achieves high lateral resolution and large-area scanning. However, such configuration cannot significantly improve the axial resolution for 3D surface measurements. The reason can be derived from the image formation theory of scanning microscopes in Fig. 3.6. The field distribution $U(x_2, y_2)$ on the image plane according to the scanning position can be represented as:

$$
\begin{aligned}
&U(x_2, y_2; x_s, y_s) \qquad (3.3)\\
&= \iint_{-\infty}^{\infty} h_1(x_0, y_0) t(x_0 - x_s, y_0 - y_s) h_2\left(\frac{x_2}{M} - x_0, \frac{y_2}{M} - y_0\right) dx_0 dy_0,
\end{aligned}
$$

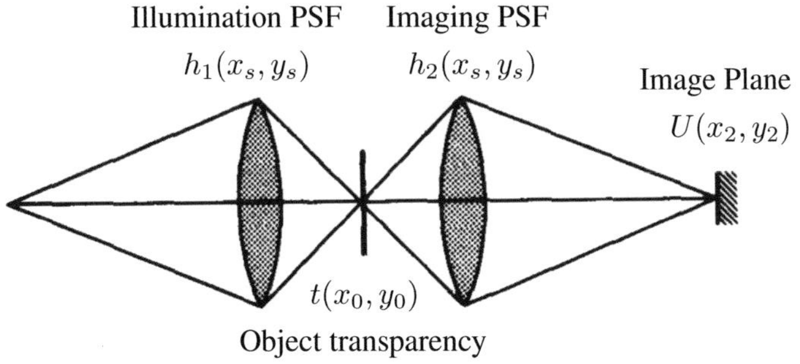

Figure 3.6: Optical configuration for a scanning microscope [WS84].

where (x_0, y_0) is the object coordinate, (x_2, y_2) is the image coordinate, (x_s, y_s) is the scanning position, $h_1(x_s, y_s)$ is the illumination point spread function (PSF), $h_2(x_s, y_s)$ is the imaging PSF, and $t(x_0, y_0)$ is the object transparency as shown in Fig. 3.6.

For a point object, the object transparency is $t(x_0, y_0) = \delta(x_0, y_0)$, and Eq. (3.3) can be simplified into:

$$
\begin{aligned}
&U(x_2, y_2; x_s, y_s) \\
&= \iint_{-\infty}^{\infty} h_1(x_0, y_0)\delta(x_0 - x_s, y_0 - y_s)h_2\left(\frac{x_2}{M} - x_0, \frac{y_2}{M} - y_0\right) dx_0 dy_0 \\
&= h_1(x_s, y_s)h_2\left(\frac{x_2}{M} - x_s, \frac{y_2}{M} - y_s\right).
\end{aligned}
\tag{3.4}
$$

For a plane object, e.g. a mirror, the object transparency is equivalent to $t(x, y) = 1$, and Eq. (3.3) can be simplified into:

$$
\begin{aligned}
&U(x_2, y_2; x_s, y_s) \\
&= \iint_{-\infty}^{\infty} h_1(x_0, y_0)h_2\left(\frac{x_2}{M} - x_0, \frac{y_2}{M} - y_0\right) dx_0 dy_0 \\
&= h_1(x_2, y_2) * h_2(x_2, y_2).
\end{aligned}
\tag{3.5}
$$

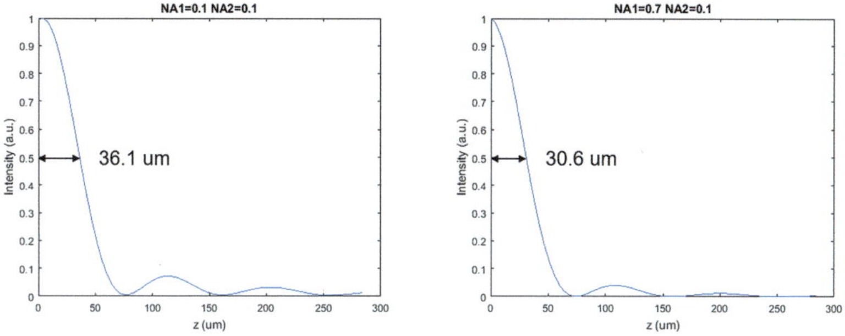

(a) Low-NA illumination and low-NA imaging.

(b) High-NA illumination and low-NA imaging.

Figure 3.7: Axial intensity responses of confocal systems for a plane object.

From Eq. (3.4) and Eq. (3.5), it is clearly shown that for a point object the response on the image plane is the product of the illumination and the imaging PSFs, while for a plane object the image is the convolution of the two PSFs. In our optical configuration with high-NA illumination and low-NA imaging, this means that for a point object, the response on the image plane will be governed by the high-NA PSF; for a plane object, it will be governed by the low-NA PSF. Thus for the 3D surface measurement, which is similar to a plane, the axial resolution cannot benefit from the high-NA illumination.

Fig. 3.7 shows simulations of axial intensity responses of confocal microscope systems for a plane object with both low-NA illumination and imaging, and with high-NA illumination and low-NA imaging respectively. The simulation setup is very simple. A spot on a mirror which is produced by an illumination lens is imaged by an imaging lens. Then the mirror is gradually moved away from the focal point and the intensity of the central pixel in the image is recorded. For both low-NA illumination and imaging, the axial half width half maximum (HWHM) is 36 µm. And with a high-NA illumination, the axial HWHM is around 30 µm. Although there is an improvement, it is not very significant and impressive.

In conclusion, such configuration in Fig. 3.3 can improve the lateral resolution by the high-NA spots produced by the DOE. However, the axial resolution is still strongly restricted by the low-NA objective. Thus it is not very suitable for 3D surface measurements.

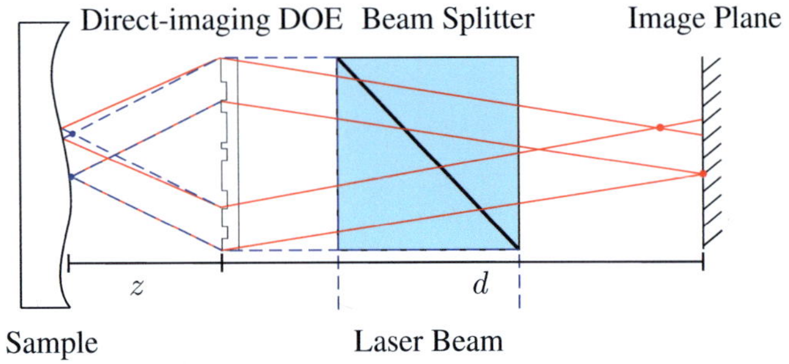

Figure 3.8: Direct-imaging configuration of a DOE-based confocal surface measurement system.

3.3 Direct-imaging DOE design

In order to increase the axial resolution and make the DOE suitable for 3D surface measurements, the optical configuration for the direct-imaging DOE design is proposed as Fig. 3.8. In this case, the DOE is the superposition of two kinds of lenses with overlapping apertures. One acts as an illumination lens which converts an incident plane wave into a spot array. The other one acts as the imaging lenses which directly image the spots onto the imaging sensor. The two lenses are overlapped as Fig. 3.1 shows. The field distribution for the new DOE is calculated again according to Eq. (3.1):

$$u_D = u_{lens1} + W u_{lens2}.$$

In this way the illumination and the imaging are both high-NA and the system can have the same performance as a high-NA confocal microscope.

Fig. 3.10 shows the simulation results with the setup in Fig. 3.8. The dashed blue lines represent the illumination light and the solid red lines represent the light refelcted from the sample. The spots are generated by the direct-imaging DOE and again imaged by itself onto the image plane. It is again optimized iteratively to achieve the highest intensities in the spot centers with the working distance $z = 1.11\,\mathrm{mm}$, the distance from the DOE to the image sensor $d = 21.262\,\mathrm{mm}$, the weighting factor $W = 0.045$ and the binarization factor $B = 0.97\pi$ in Eq. (3.2).

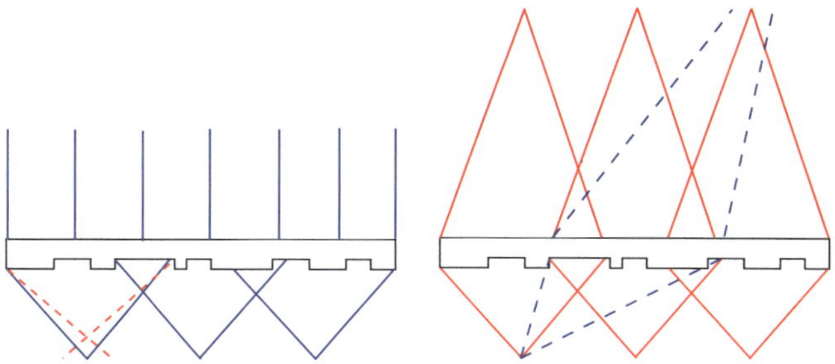

(a) Illumination through the superimposed lens

(b) Imaging through the adjacent lens.

Figure 3.9: Side effects which cause irregular interference patterns.

The pitch is 100 μm and the simulation wavelength is 785 nm. Different numbers of spots are created for the simulation. For a perfect spot on the image plane in this configuration, we calculate an ICF = 267.79. Fig. 3.10 shows a 5×5 spot array. The spots can still be seen with an ICF = 38.86. However, irregular interference patterns can already be observed in the image. When the number of spots further increases, the interference patterns will become more and more significant as in Fig. 3.10 with ICF = 19.72 and Fig. 3.10 with ICF = 5.08. The ICF drops with the increase of spot numbers. Eventually, the spots are covered by the interference patterns and they cannot be distinguished any more on the image.

These interference patterns are mainly caused by the side effects of superposition of different DOEs and overlapping apertures. As mentioned previously, the DOE is composed of two components which are generally two kinds of lenses with different focal lengths. They act as the illumination lenses and imaging lenses respectively. However, they will not work separately as we want for illumination and imaging. They will always take effect at the same time. When projecting the illumination spots, the imaging lenses will also produce a blurred spot around the spot we need, which is shown as Fig. 3.9.

Besides, on the imaging side, due to the overlapping apertures, one spot will not only pass the designed lens to form a spot on the image sensor, but also it will go through the adjacent lenses to form other blurred spots which add some disturbances to the image, which is shown in Fig. 3.9. As the number of spots increases, the image quality will reduce.

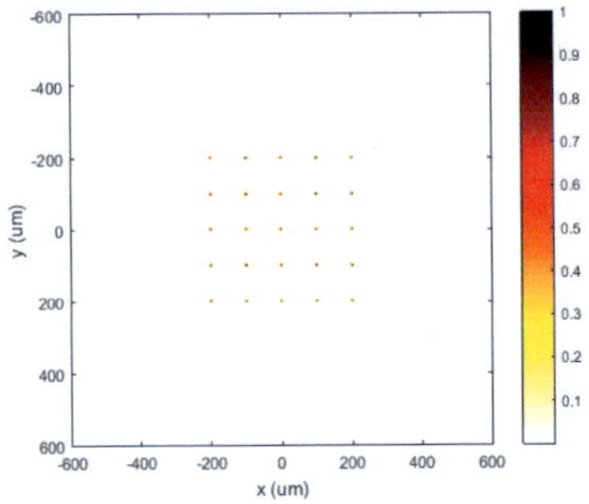

(a) 5×5 spot array on the image.

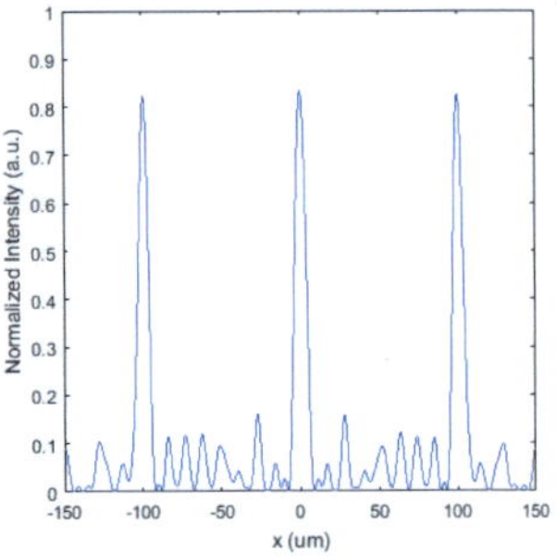

(b) Cross section at $y = 0$ in the 5×5 spot array.

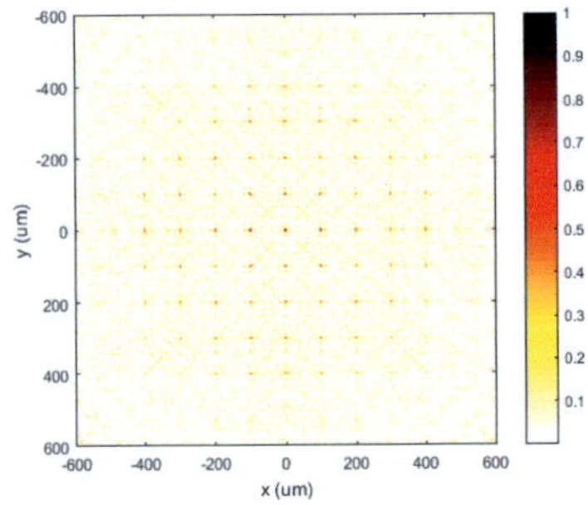

(c) 9×9 spot array on the image.

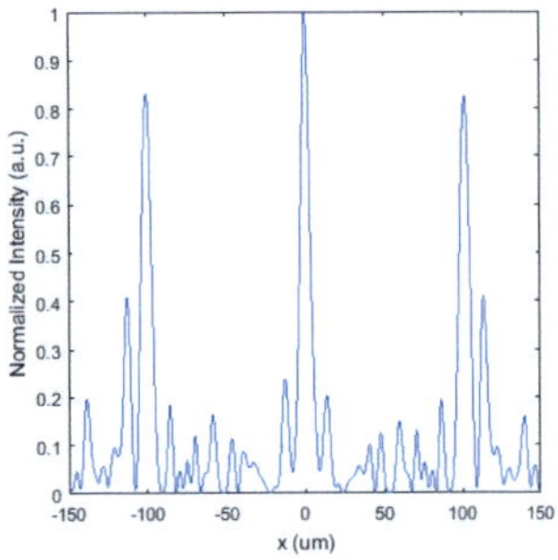

(d) Cross section at $y = 0$ in the 9×9 spot array.

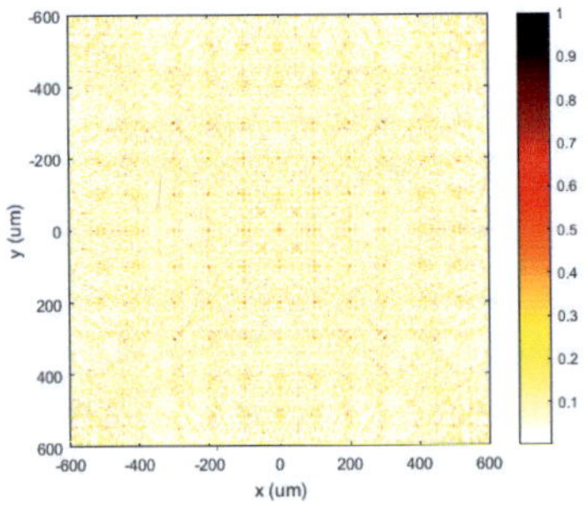

(e) 11×11 spot array on the image.

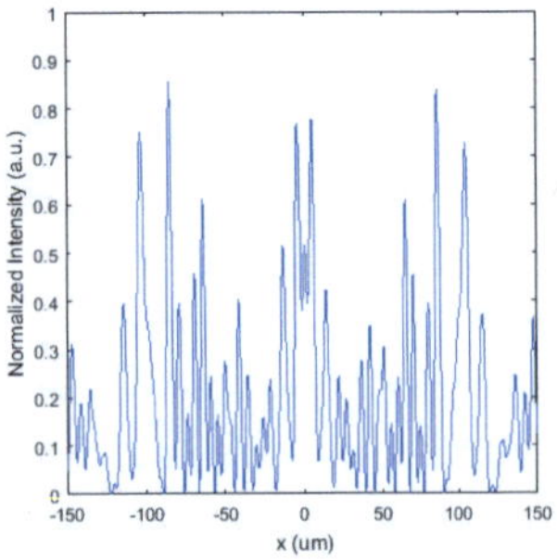

(f) Cross section at $y = 0$ in the 11×11 spot array.

Figure 3.10: Simulation of the field intensity on the image plane for the direct-imaging DOE design.

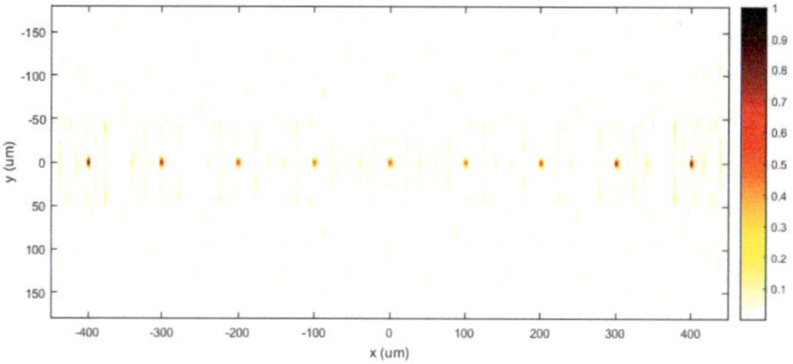

(a) The central 9 spots in a line with 21 spots on the image plane.

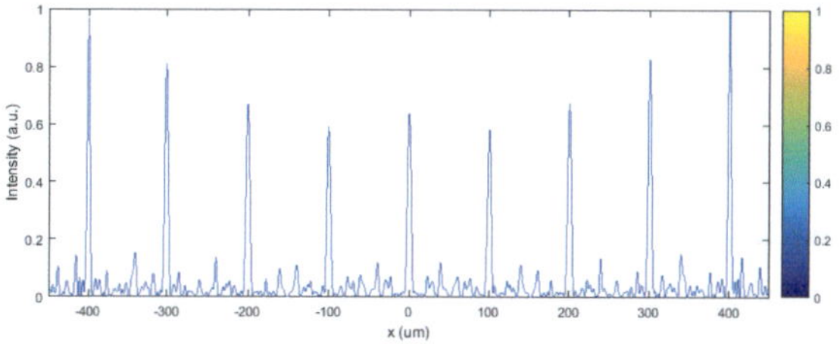

(b) Cross section of intensity profile of the line at $y = 0$.

Figure 3.11: Simulation of a spot line produced by the direct-imaging DOE.

The reason behind these side effects is too much overlapping of the elements. The overlapping can be reduced by decreasing the working distance, decreasing the NA, or increasing the pitch of the elements. However, none of these is desirable for 3D measurement. Because larger working distance, higher NA and smaller pitch are required for faster and more accurate measurement.

One possible solution could be using a line of spots instead of a 2D array to reduce the overlapping. In this case, there is no longer interference from the top and bottom spots. Meanwhile, one spot will receive less disturbances from the spots farther away. Thus the overall disturbances for a single spot can be reduced to an acceptable level and the line of spots can be extended infinitely. Fig. 3.11 shows a line of 21 spots with the working distance $z = 1.11\,\mathrm{mm}$, the distance from the DOE to the image sensor $d = 21.262\,\mathrm{mm}$, the weighting factor $W = 0.065$ and the binarization factor $B = 0.97\pi$ in Eq. (3.2). The pitch is $100\,\mu\mathrm{m}$ and the simulation wavelength is $785\,\mathrm{nm}$. As shown in the picture, the center spot receives the most disturbances from other spots but it is still clearly visible with an ICF = 32.53. And even with the increase of the spots, the central spot will receive less disturbance from the unit cells which is far away , which implies that the concept works theoretically in the simulation.

In conclusion, two DOE design concepts are proposed in this chapter. They can both produce illumination spots with an NA of 0.7 by simulation. The first see-through DOE design provides better intensity contrast with an ICF = 48.25 compared to an ideal ICF = 116.38, but it is only capable of 2D measurements. The second direct-imaging design is able to measure 3D surfaces but the number of spots is highly limited due to severe interference caused by overlapping of the components. A line scanner could be a potential solution to control the interference to an acceptable level with an ICF = 32.53 compared to an ICF = 267.79 in the ideal configuration.

4 Summary

In the current research, DOEs are used to replace high NA objectives in confocal microscopy. However, they can only measure semi-transparent samples. In this work, the ideal of superposition are proposed to overcome this limit and to enable the application of DOE for opaque surface measurements. Different methods to simulate light diffraction are compared for design the DOE. Two different DOE design concepts are simulated and investigated. Both concepts can produce an illumination spot array with an NA of 0.7. The first see-through design has a good intensity contrast on the image but it cannot provide good axial resolution. The second direct-imaging design has the same depth discerning capability as the traditional confocal microscopy. However, it suffers from low intensity contrast due to overlapping of different wave component. 1D arrangement of the spots as a line is proposed to reduce the interference and it has the potential in real industrial application.

The first piece of DOE prototype is already produced and ready for testing. In the future, experiments with the prototype will be performed to verify the simulation results, and new possibilities to use structured illumination and interference with DOEs will be investigated for 3D measurement.

Bibliography

[BGG98] Jon M Bendickson, Elias N Glytsis, and Thomas K Gaylord. Scalar integral diffraction methods: unification, accuracy, and comparison with a rigorous boundary element method with application to diffractive cylindrical lenses. *JOSA A*, 15(7):1822–1837, 1998.

[BPS+06] Eric Betzig, George H Patterson, Rachid Sougrat, O Wolf Lindwasser, Scott Olenych, Juan S Bonifacino, Michael W Davidson, Jennifer Lippincott-Schwartz, and Harald F Hess. Imaging intracellular fluorescent proteins at nanometer resolution. *Science*, 313(5793):1642–1645, 2006.

[BRS50] Henry George Booker, JA Ratcliffe, and DH Shinn. Diffraction from an irregular screen with applications to ionospheric problems. *Phil. Trans. R. Soc. Lond. A*, 242(856):579–607, 1950.

[DSS+09] Michael E. Dailey, Sidney L. Shaw, Jason R. Swedlow, Matthias F. Langhorst, and Michael W. Davidson. Microscopy techniques for live-cell imaging. `http://zeiss-campus.magnet.fsu.edu/articles/livecellimaging/techniques.html`, 2009. Online; accessed 3-November-2017.

[DZXL03] Enwen Dai, Changhe Zhou, Peng Xi, and Liren Liu. Multifunctional double-layered diffractive optical element. *Optics letters*, 28(17):1513–1515, 2003.

[Goo05] Joseph W Goodman. *Introduction to Fourier optics*. Roberts and Company Publishers, 2005.

[HVS12] Bas Hulsken, Dirk Vossen, and Sjoerd Stallinga. High NA diffractive array illuminators and application in a multi-spot scanning microscope. *Journal of the European Optical Society - Rapid publications*, 7, 2012.

[HW94] Stefan W Hell and Jan Wichmann. Breaking the diffraction resolution limit by stimulated emission: stimulated-emission-depletion fluorescence microscopy. *Optics letters*, 19(11):780–782, 1994.

[KH14] Andreas Kirsch and Frank Hettlich. *The Mathematical Theory of Maxwell's Equations*. Karlsruhe Institute of Technology (KIT), 2014.

[LB14] Xiyuan Liu and Karl-Heinz Brenner. High resolution wavefront measurement with phase retrieval using a diffractive overlapping micro lens array. In *Fringe 2013*, pages 233–236. Springer, 2014.

[Lin72] Burn Jeng Lin. Electromagnetic near-field diffraction of a medium slit. *JOSA*, 62(8):976–981, 1972.

[LSB12] Xiyuan Liu, Tim Stenau, and Karl-Heinz Brenner. Diffractive micro lens arrays with overlapping apertures. In *Information Optics (WIO), 2012 11th Euro-American Workshop on*, pages 1–2. IEEE, 2012.

[Max65] James Clerk Maxwell. A dynamical theory of the electromagnetic field. *Philosophical transactions of the Royal Society of London*, 155:459–512, 1865.

[Sil62] Samuel Silver. Microwave aperture antennas and diffraction theory. *JOSA*, 52(2):131–139, 1962.

[Som96] Arnold Sommerfeld. Mathematische theorie der diffraction. *Mathematische Annalen*, 47(2):317–374, 1896.

[Som04] Arnold Sommerfeld. *Mathematical Theory of Diffraction*. Birkhäuser Boston, Boston, MA, 2004.

[SW06] Fabin Shen and Anbo Wang. Fast-fourier-transform based numerical integration method for the rayleigh-sommerfeld diffraction formula. *Applied optics*, 45(6):1102–1110, 2006.

[VBR+15] Jeroen Vangindertael, Isabel Beets, Susana Rocha, Peter Dedecker, Liliane Schoofs, Karen Vanhoorelbeke, Johan Hofkens, and Hideaki Mizuno. Super-resolution mapping of glutamate receptors in c. elegans by confocal correlated palm. *Scientific reports*, 5:13532, 2015.

[Voe11] David George Voelz. *Computational fourier optics: a MATLAB tutorial*. SPIE press Bellingham, WA, 2011.

[WS84] Tony Wilson and Colin Sheppard. *Theory and practice of scanning optical microscopy*, volume 180. Academic Press London, 1984.

[Zhe16] Guoan Zheng. *Fourier Ptychographic Imaging: A Matlab Tutorial*. Morgan & Claypool Publishers, 2016.

Industrial Network Topology Analysis with Episode Mining

Ankush Meshram

Vision and Fusion Laboratory
Institute for Anthropomatics
Karlsruhe Institute of Technology (KIT), Germany
ankush.meshram@kit.edu

Technical Report IES-2018-04

Abstract

Industrial network communication is highly deterministic as result of availability requirement of control systems in automated industrial production systems. This deterministic character helps with initial step of self-learning anomaly detection systems to detect periodic production cycle in industrial network communication. The methods for frequent episode mining in event sequences fits well to solve the challenge of production cycle detection for self-learning system. We encode the network communication events to serial and parallel episodes. Methods for discovery of frequent episodes in event sequences are briefly explained. These methods would be further adapted in future to our encoded network communication traffic to extract production cycle comprised of serial and parallel episodes.

1 Introduction

Industrial network communication enforces high availability requirement for automated industrial production systems. This results into deterministic and discrete communication behaviour between network components, and hence industrial control system components [Mes17]. The foremost task for self-learning anomaly detection in industrial networks is detecting the periodic synchronous communication resulting from the production cycle of the industrial

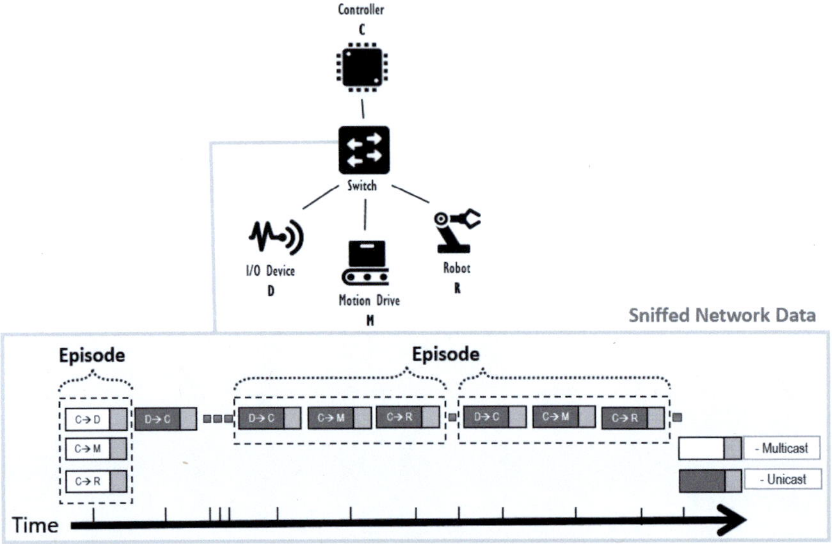

Figure 1.1: Example Drilling System.

system[MH16]. In order to do so the network communication traffic is sniffed and analyzed to detect the production cycle.

In this report, we propose the usage of Episode Mining paradigm to discover periodic patterns in the network traffic sequence [MTV97]. In the following sections, we begin with requirements for production cycle detection in industrial networks with a sample scenario in Section 2. Then, we map the industrial communication events to Episode and its variants in Section 3. We briefly explain the different methodologies for frequent episode mining.

2 Production Cycle Detection in Industrial Networks

For production cycle detection, we analyze the continuous sequential network communication traffic data. Our goal is to extract periodic patterns from the analyzed traffic while preserving the time order of communication events. Network

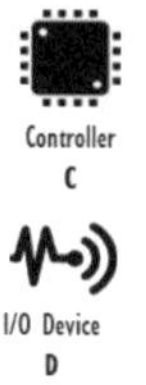

MAC	03:9C:45:34:8F	M1
IP	172.65.21.7	I1
Port	502 (TCP)	P1

MAC	88:9F:59:04:4C	M2
IP	172.65.21.26	I2
Port	46176 (TCP)	P2

Protocol Encoding	
Ethernet	E00
Profinet	P00
IP	I00
TCP (SYN)	T08
TCP (SYN-ACK)	T58
TCP (ACK)	T05

Figure 2.1: Mapping of component properties (MAC Address, IP Address and Port Number) and Protocol Flags to text variables.

communication at higher levels does not happen in isolation. For example, when OSI Layer 4 protocol TCP is used for communicating information from one node to another, the underlying Layer 3 and Layer 2 protocols also participate simultaneously. Hence, we need pattern extraction method which considers strict or partial ordering of simultaneous events.

We consider an example scenario of simple drilling system as depicted in Figure 1.1. The I/O Device (D) notifies PLC controller (C) that a metal block has arrived on conveyor belt driven by a Motor (M). The Controller then signals the Motor to run for a fixed time duration and move metal block under the Drilling Robot (R). After the fixed time has passed, Controller signals Robot to drill a hole in the metal block. This whole process repeats itself and is the production cycle we want to detect from network traffic, sniffed at Switch (S) without any further information about industrial setup.

We found a solution in the Episode Mining framework where our periodic patterns are called episodes. An episode is a partially ordered collection of events occurring together as defined in [MTV97]. We explain further in the next section discovery of Episode as the appropriate periodic pattern extraction method for production cycle detection in industrial network communication.

3 Episode Mining for Production Cycle Detection

To understand Episodes further we consider the communication between components Controller (C) and I/O Device (D) with respective information of MAC-address, IP-address and Port with type. For easier explanation, we encode the device information with text variables. MAC addresses are mapped to variables beginning with '**M**' and appropriate indexing. Similarly, IP addresses and Port are mapped to variables beginning with '**I**' and '**P**' followed by appropriate indexing respectively. Also we follow an encoding scheme for protocols through which these devices might communicate. The last two digit represents the state of stateful protocol. In particular, successful TCP-Handshake communication follows SYN, SYN-ACK and ACK. Figure 2.1 lists up the mappings for Controller and I/O Device with protocol encoding for Ethernet, Profinet and TCP communication protocols.

The observed network traffic is complex. Each packet contains information on communication occurring at multiple OSI Layers. For explanation we consider here only L2 to L4 communication and encode the communication contained in the packet. The higher layer communication doesn't happen in isolation as mentioned earlier. For example, in Figure 3.1, the third packet communicated between Controller and I/O Device, the encoding '**P1P2T08**' represents Port P1 of Controller initiated TCP-Handshake with Port P2 of Device, along with communication at L3 and L2 encoded as '**I1I2I00**' and '**M1M2P00**'. Events following a total order are called Serial Episode whereas these ones following trivial order are called Parallel Episodes. In Figure 3.1, {**M1M2P00, M2M1P00**} is a Serial Episode and { **P1P2T08 I1I2I00 M1M2P00** } is a Parallel Episode. In particular two events marked with thick-edged rectangle could be TCP SYN flooding attack as the TCP Handshake is initiated again.

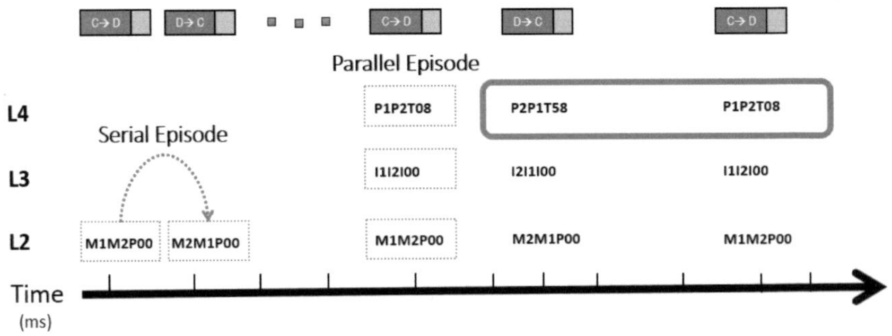

Figure 3.1: Mapped network traffic to Episodes.

More formally, episode mining can be described as follows with basic definitions. Given a set of event types E, an event is a pair (A,t) where $A \in E$ is an event type and t is an integer representing time of occurrence. An Event Sequence **s** is a triple (s, T_s, T_e) with ordered sequence of events A_i and T_s representing starting time, T_e representing ending time. The event occurring at ending time isn't included in the sequence.

$$s = \langle (A_1, T_1), (A_2, T_2), .., (A_n, T_n) \rangle$$
$$\text{s.t. } A_i \in E \forall i = 1, .., n \text{ and } t_i \leq t_{i+1} \forall i = 1, .., n-1$$
$$T_s \leq t_i < T_e \forall i = 1, .., n$$

The window of Figure 3.2 is a slice of event sequence and an event sequence can be considered as a sequence of partially overlapping windows. A window on an event sequence $\mathbf{s} = (s, T_s, T_e)$ is an event sequence $\mathbf{w} = (w, t_s, t_e)$ such that $t_s < T^e$ and $t_e > T_s$. The width of window **w** is defined by $width(\mathbf{w}) = win = t_e - t_s$. $W(\mathbf{s}, w)$ is a set of all windows **w** on event sequence **s** given window width win. The number of windows in $W(\mathbf{s}, win)$ is calculated as $T_e - T_s - win + 1$.

An episode α is a triple $(V, \leq, g)$ such that V is set of nodes, $\leq$ is partial order on V, and g is mapping associating each node with an event type i.e. $g : V \rightarrow E$. The size of episode α is defined by $|V|$. Episode α is parallel if relation $\leq$ is trivial i.e. $x \nleq y, \forall x, y \in V \text{s.t.} x \neq y$. Episode α is serial if relation $\leq$ is total order i.e. $x \leq y$ or $y \leq x, \forall x, y \in V$.

An episode $\beta = (V^{'}, \leq^{'}, g^{'})$ is a *subepisode* of $\alpha = (V, \leq, g)$ i.e. $\beta \preceq \alpha$ if $\exists f : V^{'} \rightarrow V$ s.t. $g^{'}(v) = g(f(v)) \forall v \in V^{'}$ and $\forall v, w \in V^{'}$ with $v \leq^{'} w$ also $f(v) \leq f(w)$. An episode α is *superepisode* of β i.e. $\beta \prec \alpha$ **if and only if** $\beta \preceq \alpha$.

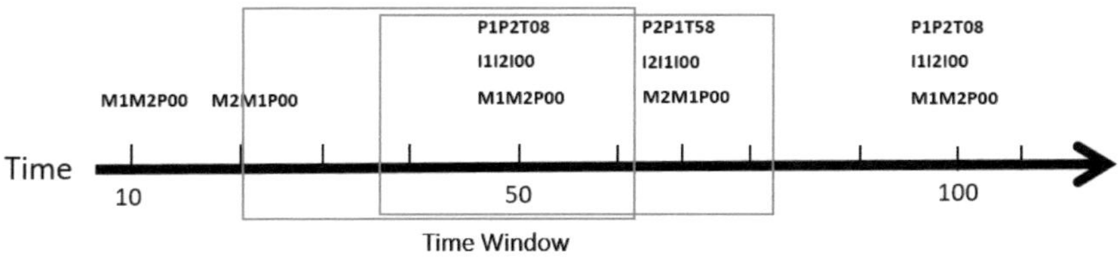

Figure 3.2: Windows for Episode Mining.

Algorithm 3.1 WINEPI Algorithm

Input: A set E of event types, an event sequence s over E,
a set ε of episodes, a window width win, and a frequency threshold min_fr

Output: The collection $\mathfrak{F}(s, win, min\_fr)$ of frequent episodes.

Method:

```
C_1 := {α ∈ ε | |α| = 1}
l := 1
while C_l ≠ ∅ do
    compute 𝔉_l := {α ∈ C_l | fr(α, s, win) ≥ min_fr};
    l := l + 1;
    compute C_l := {α ∈ ε | |α| = l and for all β ∈ ε
                     such that β ≺ α and |β| < l we have β ∈ 𝔉_|β|}
end while
for all l do
    output 𝔉_l;
end for
```

An episode $\alpha = (V, \leq, g)$ occurs in an event sequence $\mathbf{s} = (\langle (A_1, T_1), (A_2, T_2), .., (A_n, T_n) \rangle, T_s, T_e)$, if $\exists h : V \rightarrow \{1, .., n\}$ from nodes of α to events of **s** s.t. $g(s) = A_{h(x)} \forall x, y \in V$ with $x \neq y$ and $x \leq y$ we have $t_{h(x)} < t_{h(y)}$.

Frequency of an episode given an event sequence and window width is ratio of number of windows of the set of all windows on sequence in which it occurs to total number of windows on sequence. Frequency of an episode α in an event sequence **s** with window width win,

$$fr(\alpha, \mathbf{s}, win) = \frac{|\{w \in W(s, win)\} \, | \alpha \; occurs \; in \; w|}{|W(\mathbf{s}, win))|}$$

For a given frequency threshold min_fr, α is **frequent** if $fr(\alpha, \mathbf{s}, win) \geq min\_fr$.

The mining task is given an event sequence **s**, a window width win and a frequency threshold min_fr, discover all frequent episodes from a class ε of episodes - $\mathfrak{F}(\mathbf{s}, win, min\_fr)$. WINEPI algorithm 3.1 listed below discovers frequent episodes from an event sequence. Alternate approach to sliding window based

WINEPI is MINEPI algorithm. MINEPI is based on minimal occurrences of episodes where for each potentially interesting episode we find out the exact occurrences of the episode. One disadvantage to WINEPI is that MINEPI consumes significant amount of space. WINEPI and MINEPI work on offline dataset of sequences, MESELO [ALL+15] is an algorithm for online frequent episode mining. MESELO stands for 'Mining frEquent Serial Episode via Last Occurrence' where authors introduced sophisticated data structure, *episode trie*, to store minimal occurrences of episodes compactly.

4 Summary

This report outlines using Episode Mining for Production Cycle Detection in Industrial Network Communication. A mapping for communication events to text variables is explained which are used later on to detect Serial and Parallel Episodes. Different methods for frequent episode mining are available. Implementation of MESELO algorithm modified for our goal is underway.

Bibliography

[ALL+15] Xiang Ao, Ping Luo, Chengkai Li, Fuzhen Zhuang, and Qing He. Online frequent episode mining. In *2015 IEEE 31st International Conference on Data Engineering (ICDE)*, pages 891–902. IEEE, 2015.

[Mes17] Ankush Meshram. Deterministic industrial network communication: Fundamentals. In Jürgen Beyerer, Alexey Pak, and Miro Taphanel, editors, *Joint Workshop of Fraunhofer IOSB and Institute for Anthropomatics, Vision and Fusion Laboratory 2017. Proceedings*, pages 45–61, Triberg-Nussbach, July 2017. Karlsruhe: KIT Scientific Publishing, 2018 (Karlsruher Schriften zur Anthropomatik 34).

[MH16] Ankush Meshram and Christian Haas. Anomaly detection in industrial networks using machine learning: A roadmap. In *Machine Learning for Cyber Physical Systems 2016*, pages 65–72, Karlsruhe, Germany, September 2016.

[MTV97] Heikki Mannila, Hannu Toivonen, and A Inkeri Verkamo. Discovery of frequent episodes in event sequences. *Data mining and knowledge discovery*, 1(3):259–289, 1997.

RNN-based Prediction of Pedestrian Turning Maneuvers

Stefan Becker

Fraunhofer Institute for Optronics,
System Technologies, and Image Exploitation IOSB
Gutleuthausstr. 1, 76275 Ettlingen, Germany
stefan.becker@iosb.fraunhofer.de

Technical Report IES-2018-05

Abstract

The dynamics of objects, such as pedestrians, varies over time. Commonly this problem is tackled with traditional approaches like the Interacting Multiple Model (IMM) filter using a Bayesian formulation. Following the current trend towards using deep neural networks, in this paper an RNN-based alternative solution for pedestrian maneuver prediction is presented. Similar to an IMM filter solution, the presented model assigns a confidence value to a performed dynamic and, based on them, puts out a multi-modal distribution over future pedestrian trajectories. The qualitative evaluation is done on synthetic data, reflecting prototypical pedestrian maneuvers.

1 Introduction

The applications of pedestrian path prediction cover a wide range from robot navigation, autonomous driving, smart video surveillance to object tracking. Traditionally, the task of object motion prediction is addressed by using a Bayesian Formulation in approaches such as the Kalman filter [Kal60], or nonparametric methods, such as particle filters [AMGC02]. Following the success of recurrent neural networks (RNNs) in modeling temporal dependencies in a variety

of sequence processing tasks, such as speech recognition [GMH13, CKD+15] and caption generation [DHG+15, XBK+15], RNNs are increasingly utilized for object motion prediction [AGR+16, ARG+17, HBHA17, HBHA18, BHHA18]. When relying on traditional approaches, the challenge of changing dynamics over time or rather maneuvers is commonly done with the Interacting Multiple Model (IMM) filter [BBS88]. The IMM filter is an elegant way to combine a set of candidate models into a single context by weighting each individual model. Each model corresponds to a specific motion pattern and contributes to the final state estimation depending on its current weight. According to the IMM filter solution, in this paper an RNN-based model is presented, which on the one hand is able to also provide a confidence value for the performed dynamic and on the other hand can overcome some limitations of the IMM filter. The suggested RNN-encoder-decoder model generates the probability distribution over future pedestrian paths conditioned on a maneuver class. The model is based on the work of Deo and Trivedi [DT18]. For the case of freeway traffic, they used an RNN-encoder-decoder network for vehicle maneuver and trajectory prediction. In the context of vehicle motion prediction, maneuver classes can be better defined than for pedestrians. Due to the dynamic behavior of pedestrians, the maneuver classes are here defined based on the deviation of a straight walking pedestrian. The presented network adapts the maneuver network of Deo and Trivedi with insights of the work of Becker et al. [BHHA18] for RNN-based pedestrian trajectory prediction. The analysis is done on synthetic data reflecting prototypical scenarios capturing turning maneuvers of pedestrians.
In the following, a brief formalization of the problem and a description of the RNN-based model are provided. The qualitative achieved results are presented in section 3. Finally, a conclusion is given in section 4.

2 RNN-based Pedestrian Maneuver Prediction

The goal is to devise a model that can successfully predict future paths of pedestrians and represent alternating pedestrian dynamics, e.g. dynamics that can transition from a straight walking to a turning maneuver. Here, trajectory prediction is formally stated as the problem of predicting the future trajectories of a pedestrian, conditioned on its track history. Given an input sequence $\mathcal{O} = \{(x^t, y^t) \in \mathbb{R}^2 | t = 1, \ldots, t_{obs}\}$ of T_{obs} consecutive pedestrian positions $\vec{x}^t = (x^t, y^t)$ at time

t along a trajectory the task is to generate a multi-modal prediction for the next T_{pred} positions $\{\vec{x}^{t+1}, \vec{x}^{t+2}, \ldots, \vec{x}^{t+T_{pred}}\}$. One insight of the work Becker et al. [BHHA18] is that motion continuity is easier to express in offsets or velocities, because it takes considerably more modeling effort to represent all possible conditioning positions. For exploiting scene-specific knowledge for trajectory prediction, additional use of the position information is required. When sufficient training samples from a particular scene are available, Hug et al.[HBHA17] showed that RNN-based trajectory prediction models are able to capture spatially depending behavior changes only from motion data. However, here the offsets are used for conditioning the network $\mathcal{O} = \{(\delta_x^t, \delta_y^t) \in \mathbb{R}^2 | t = 2, \ldots, t_{obs}\}$. Apart from the smaller modeling effort to represent conditioned offsets, the shift to offsets helps to prevent undefined states due to a limited data range [BHHA18]. Furthermore, it is easier to capture the scene-independent aspect of human behavior and to better generalize across datasets. The future trajectory is denoted with $\mathcal{Y} = \{(x^t, y^t) \in \mathbb{R}^2 | t = t_{obs} + 1, \ldots, t_{pred}\}$ and the model estimates the conditional distribution $P(\mathcal{Y}|\mathcal{O})$. In order to identify specific dynamics under M desired maneuver classes (e.g. turning maneuvers and straight walking), this term can be given by:

$$P(\mathcal{Y}|\mathcal{O}) = \sum_{i}^{M} P_{\Theta}(\mathcal{Y}|m_i, \mathcal{O}) P(m_i|\mathcal{O})$$

Here, $\Theta = \{\Theta^{t_{obs}+1}, \ldots, \Theta^{t_{pred}}\}$ are the parameters of a L component Gaussian mixture model $\Theta^t = (\vec{\mu}_l^t, \Sigma_l^t, w_l^t)_{l=1,\ldots,L}$. By adding the maneuver context in form of the posterior mode probability, $P(m_i|\mathcal{O}) \triangleq \alpha_i$ the analogy to the classic IMM filter becomes apparent. For an IMM filter the mode probability is used to calculate the mixing probabilities to combine the set of chosen candidate models into a merged estimate. In case of using an IMM filter the time behavior of the basic filter set is modeled as a homogeneous (time invariant) Markov chain with a fixed transition probability matrix (TPM) $m_{ij} \triangleq P(m_i^t | m_j^{t-1})$. Instead of setting the parameter of the time behavior manually, the current mode probability is inferred from the hidden states of the RNN. For the proposed RNN-based pedestrian maneuver prediction model, the basic architecture is a Recurrent-Encoder-Decoder model. The encoder takes the frame by frame input sequence $\mathcal{O}$. The hidden state vector of the encoder is updated at each time step based on the previous hidden state and the current offset. The generated internal representation is used to predict mode probability $\vec{\alpha}^t$ at the current time step. The encoder can be defined as follows:

$$\begin{aligned}\vec{h}^t_{encoder} &= \text{RNN}(\vec{h}^{t-1}_{encoder}, \vec{\delta}^t_{(x,y)}; W_{encoder})\\ \vec{\alpha}^t_{logits} &= \text{MLP}(\vec{h}^t_{encoder}; W_{en})\\ \hat{\vec{\alpha}}^t &= \frac{\exp(\vec{\alpha}^t_{logits})}{\sum_{j=1}^{M}\exp(\alpha^t_{logits,j})}\end{aligned}$$

Here, $RNN(\cdot)$ is the recurrent network, $\vec{h}$ the hidden state of the RNN and $MLP(\cdot)$ the multilayer perceptron. W represents the weights and biases of the MLP or respectively RNN. The final state of the encoder can be expected to encode information about the track histories. For generating a trajectory distribution over dynamic modes, the encoder hidden state is appended with a one-hot encoded vector corresponding to specific maneuvers. Hence the network is conditioned purely on offsets, position information is required to localize. Localization information persists here only implicitly by performing path integration and using the last observed point $\vec{x}^{t_{obs}}$ as reference point. The decoder of the model can be defined as follows:

$$\begin{aligned}\vec{h}^t_{decoder} &= \text{RNN}(\vec{h}^{t-1}_{decoder}[\vec{h}^t_{encoder}], \vec{\alpha}^t; W_{decoder})\\ \hat{\mathcal{Y}} = \{(\hat{\vec{\mu}}^t_l + \vec{x}^{t_{obs}}, \hat{\Sigma}^t_l, \hat{w}^t_l)|t &= t_{obs}+1, \ldots, t_{pred}\} = \text{MLP}(\vec{h}^t_{decoder}; W_{de})\end{aligned}$$

The decoder is used to parametrize a mixture density output layer (MDL) or rather Θ directly for several positions in the future. Nevertheless, the overall RNN-based pedestrian maneuver prediction network uses the trajectory prediction and dynamic classification jointly, the loss function for training is splitted into two parts. Dynamic classification is trained to mimimize the sum of cross-entropy losses of the different M motion model classes:

$$\mathcal{L}(\mathcal{O})_{maneuver} = -\sum_{j=1}^{M} \alpha^t_{j,GT}\log(\hat{\alpha}^t_j)$$

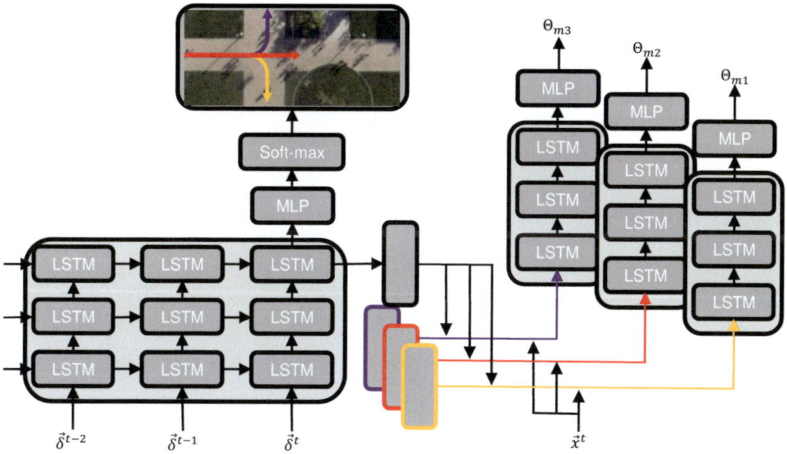

Figure 2.1: Visualization of the RNN-encoder-decoder network for jointly predicting specific dynamic probabilities and corresponding future distributions of trajectory positions. The encoder predicts the dynamic or rather maneuver probabilities and the decoder uses the context vector to predict future pedestrian locations.

Additionally, the encoder-decoder is trained by minimizing the negative log likelihood for the ground truth future pedestrian locations conditioned under the performed maneuver class. The context vector is appended with the ground truth values of the maneuver classes for each training trajectory. This results in the following loss function:

$$\mathcal{L}(\mathcal{O})_{pred} = -\log(P_\Theta(\hat{\mathcal{Y}}|m_{GT}, \mathcal{O})P(m_{GT}|\mathcal{O}))$$

$$\mathcal{L}(\mathcal{O})_{pred} = \sum_{t=t_{obs}+1}^{t_{pred}} -\log(\sum_{l=1}^{L} \hat{w}_l^t \mathcal{N}(\vec{x}^t|\hat{\vec{\mu}}_l^t + \vec{x}^{t_{obs}}, \hat{\Sigma}_l^t; m_{GT}))$$

The overall architecture is visualized in figure 2.1. The context vector combines the encoding of the track history with the encoding of the alternating dynamic classes and is used as input for the decoder.

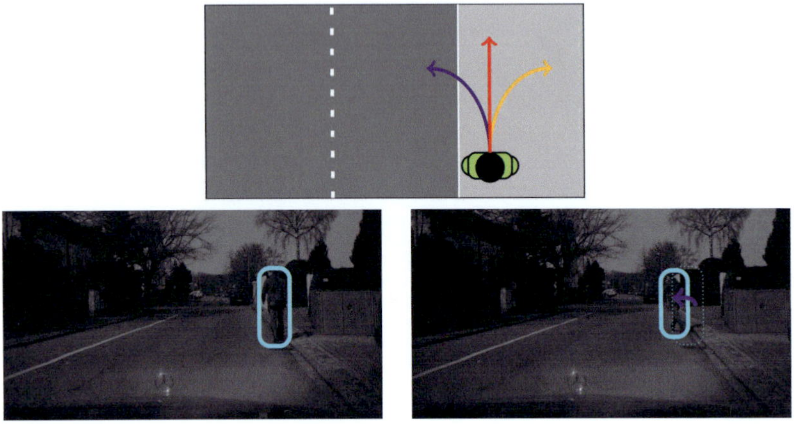

Figure 3.1: Illustration of a typical pedestrian motion. The above image images depicts the three chosen maneuver classes of straight walking and taking a turn to the left or the right. The images below show a person changing from straight walking to crossing the street complying to a change from the defined maneuver classes. In particular from straight walking to turning left. In the context of intelligent vehicles, this is often called bending in [SG13].

3 Data Generation and Evaluation

This section consists of a brief qualitative evaluation of the proposed approach. The evaluation is concerned with verifying the overall viability of the approach in maneuver situations. For initial results, a synthetic test condition is used in order to gain insight into the model behavior in different typical pedestrian motion types. A prototypical maneuver performed by a pedestrian with keen interest in the context of intelligent vehicles and video surveillance is a turning maneuver. In such a maneuver the dynamics of a pedestrian changes from a straight walking into a bending in behavior. So long as a person moves in a straight line at a reasonably constant speed, its dynamics can be captured with a Kalman filter and a constant velocity model. During the maneuver, the relation to one fixed process model describing the dynamics fails. In the context of modeling the dynamics of pedestrians this switch in dynamics is normally modeled with an IMM filter. For example in the work of Schneider et al. [SG13] or Kooij et al. [KSFG14], the motion of pedestrians is modeled with an IMM filter combining basic models like constant velocity and constant acceleration model. In such a situation the motion changes from a rectilinear dynamic to a curvilinear motion, in relation to the dynamic this results in an additional acceleration. Therefore, a change from a constant velocity model to a turning model or acceleration model indicates a critical situation from the vehicle perspective. Figure 3.1 illustrates such a turning maneuver.

For generating synthetic trajectories of a basic maneuvering pedestrian, random agents are sampled from a Gaussian distribution according to the preferred pedestrian walking speed [Tek02] ($\mathcal{N}(1,38\frac{m}{s}, 0.37\frac{m}{s})$). During a single trajectory simulation the agents can perform a turning maneuver. For the presented results the turning event takes 5 steps for a $90°$ change in heading with a fixed frame rate of 1 frame per second. The observation noise of the position sensor is assumed to be Gaussian distributed in x and y with $\sigma = 0.2m$. As mentioned above, a definition of maneuver class for pedestrians is harder to establish than for vehicles. Here, the main interest is here to detect a deviation from a standard behavior, and whether the pedestrian is in a *normal* mode. A set deviation in heading for a required time horizon can then be used to assign maneuver labels to single trajectories. As the distribution over the trajectories is captured with a Gaussian mixture model the maneuver description for the outlier trajectory distribution can still be multi-modal. For the *normal* or straight motion a single Gaussian component is sufficient. In case of the generated synthetic data, the turning maneuver trajectory distribution could be captured using one Gaussian component.

The model has been implemented using *Tensorflow* [Aba15] and is trained for 300 epochs using ADAM optimizer [KB15] with a fixed learning rate of 0.003. For the experiments the RNN variant Long Short-Term Memory [HS97] (LSTM) is used. In figure 3.2 predictions for three different preformed motion types are depicted. In all shown images the maneuver has started two time steps before. The resulting multi-modal prediction is visualized as a heatmap for the images on the left. On the right, the visualization shows the predicted covariances for 12 future positions weighted by the predicted maneuver probability and temporally. Turning to the left is highlighted in purple, walking straight with red and turning to the right in yellow.

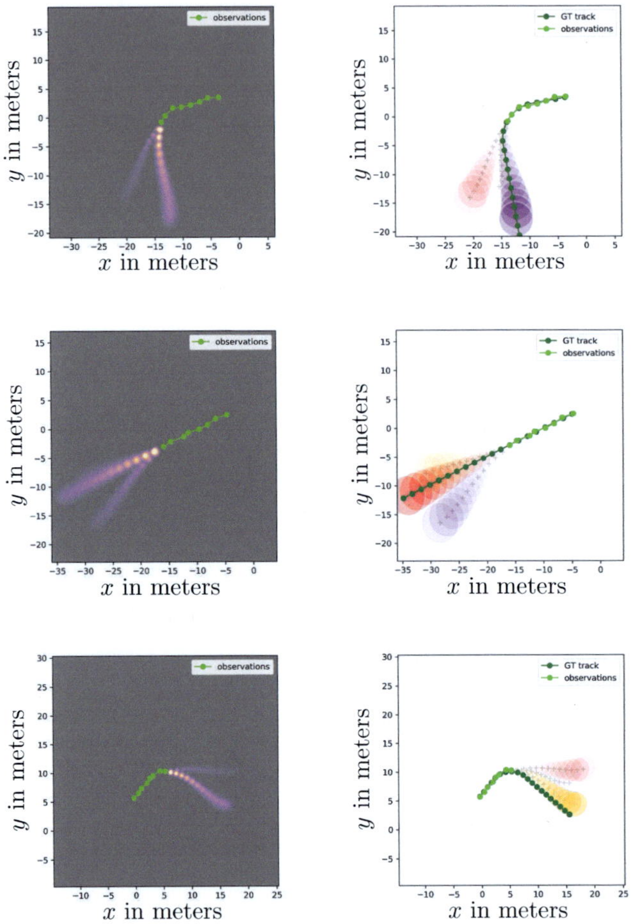

Figure 3.2: Visualization of the multi-modal predictions of the network. (Left) Density plots of the three different maneuvers. (Right) Visualization of the predicted covariance matrices with a temporal weighting and depending on the estimated maneuver probability. The turning maneuver predictions are visualized in purple and respectively yellow. The predictions for straight walking are highlighted in red.

The shown results are achieved based on noisy observations. The model is able to successfully recognize the turning behavior and to produce a reasonable distribution for the further positions. Without the explicit splitting into maneuver classes, an RNN-based solution which generates a Gaussian mixture model condition on the input sequence, is also capable to produce a similar multi-modal distribution (see for example the work of Hug et al. [HBHA17]). However, the presented model is able to successfully assign probabilities to current performed pedestrian behavior instead of only encoding this information in the hidden states of the RNN. Similar to the provided mode probabilities of IMM filters this can be used for further processing steps. Thus, the presented RNN-based model is able to also provide a confidence value $P(m_i|\mathcal{O}) \triangleq \alpha_i$ for the performed dynamic, but to avoid modeling the dynamic transitions with a fixed transition probability matrix $P(m_i^t|m_j^{t-1})$. Further, instead of choosing the basic filter set, the prediction model is learned. In case there exists some well known model for describing the standard dynamic of the desired target, only deviations from the known dynamic can be used to define additional maneuver classes.

4 Conclusion

In this report, an RNN-encoder-decoder model aimed to jointly predicting specific dynamic probabilities and corresponding distributions of future pedestrian trajectory has been presented. The model capabilities were shown on synthetic data reflecting typical pedestrian maneuvers. By conditioning on specific dynamic models or rather deviation of standard behavior, the model makes it possible to generate additional information in terms of an assigned maneuver probability similar to an IMM filter, but without the explicit modeling of the dynamic transitions.

Bibliography

[Aba15] M. Abadi et al. TensorFlow: Large-scale machine learning on heterogeneous systems, 2015. Software available from tensorflow.org.

[AGR+16] A. Alahi, K. Goel, V. Ramanathan, A. Robicquet, L. Fei-Fei, and S. Savarese. Social LSTM: Human trajectory prediction in crowded spaces. In *Conference on Computer Vision and Pattern Recognition (CVPR)*, pages 961–971. IEEE, 2016.

[AMGC02] M.S. Arulampalam, S. Maskell, N. Gordon, and T. Clapp. A tutorial on particle filters for online nonlinear/non-gaussian bayesian tracking. *Transactions on Signal Processing*, 50(2):174–188, 2002.

[ARG+17] A. Alahi, V. Ramanathan, K. Goel, A. Robicquet, A. Sadeghian, L. Fei-Fei, and S. Savarese. Learning to predict human behaviour in crowded scenes. In *Group and Crowd Behavior for Computer Vision*. Elsevier, 2017.

[BBS88] H.A.P. Blom and Y. Bar-Shalom. The interacting multiple model algorithm for systems with markovian switching coefficients. *Transactions on Automatic Control*, 33(8):780–783, 1988.

[BHHA18] S. Becker, R. Hug, W. Hübner, and M. Arens. Red: A simple but effective baseline predictor for the trajnet benchmark. In *European Conference on Computer Vision (ECCV) Workshops*. Springer International Publishing, 2018.

[CKD+15] J. Chung, K. Kastner, L. Dinh, K. Goel, A. Courville, and Y. Bengio. A recurrent latent variable model for sequential data. In *Advances in Neural Information Processing Systems (NIPS)*, 2015.

[DHG+15] J. Donahue, L.A. Hendricks, S. Guadarrama, M. Rohrbach, S. Venugopalan, K. Saenko, and T. Darrell. Long-term recurrent convolutional networks for visual recognition and description. In *Conference on Computer Vision and Pattern Recognition (CVPR)*. IEEE, 2015.

[DT18] N. Deo and M.M. Trivedi. Multi-modal trajectory prediction of surrounding vehicles with maneuver based lstms. In *Intelligent Vehicles Symposium (IV)*, pages 1179–1184. IEEE, 2018.

[GMH13] A. Graves, A.R. Mohamed, and G. Hinton. Speech recognition with deep recurrent neural networks. In *International Conference on Acoustics, Speech and Signal Processing*, pages 6645–6649, 2013.

[HBHA17] R. Hug, S. Becker, W. Hübner, and M. Arens. On the reliability of LSTM-MDL models for pedestrian trajectory prediction. In *Representations, Analysis and Recognition of Shape and Motion from Imaging Data (RFMI)*, Savoie, France, 2017.

[HBHA18] R. Hug, S. Becker, W. Hübner, and M. Arens. Particle-based pedestrian path prediction using LSTM-MDL models. In *21st International Conference on Intelligent Transportation Systems (ITSC)*, pages 2684–2691, 2018.

[HS97] S. Hochreiter and J. Schmidhuber. Long Short-Term Memory. *Neural Computation*, 9(8):1735–1780, 1997.

[Kal60] R.E. Kalman. A new approach to linear filtering and prediction problems. *ASME Journal of Basic Engineering*, 82, 1960.

[KB15] D.P. Kingma and J. Ba. Adam: A method for stochastic optimization. *International Conference for Learning Representations (ICLR)*, 2015.

[KSFG14] J.F.P. Kooij, N. Schneider, F. Flohr, and D.M. Gavrila. Context-based pedestrian path prediction. In *European Conference on Computer Vision (ECCV)*, pages 618–633. Springer International Publishing, 2014.

[SG13] N. Schneider and D.M. Gavrila. Pedestrian path prediction with recursive bayesian filters: A comparative study. In *German Conference on Pattern Recognition (GCPR)*, pages 174–183. Springer Berlin Heidelberg, 2013.

[Tek02] K. Teknom. *Microscopic Pedestrian Flow Characteristics: Development of an Image Processing Data Collection and Simulation Model.* PhD thesis, Tohoku University, 2002.

[XBK+15] K. Xu, J. Ba, R. Kiros, K.Cho, A. Courville, R. Salakhudinov, R. Zemel, and Y. Bengio. Show, attend and tell: Neural image caption generation with visual attention. In *International Conference on Machine Learning (ICML)*, volume 37, pages 2048–2057, Lille, France, 2015. PMLR.

A Game-Theoretic Framework for Safety and Security

Tim Zander

Vision and Fusion Laboratory
Institute for Anthropomatics
Karlsruhe Institute of Technology (KIT), Germany
tim.zander@kit.edu

Technical Report IES-2018-06

Abstract

The purpose of this paper is to describe the Framework described in [BG16] in a game theoretic way. The idea behind this is that for modelling security (i. e. the assumption of an intelligent attacker) the language of game theory seems to be a very good choice. Game theory can deal with the problem where the actions of each subject are interdependent, e.g. an attacker will change his strategy whenever a new security feature will prevent his old strategy from succeeding or a new attack seems to be more promising. Moreover, game theory has been thoroughly studied and hence changing the description language of the model, gives access to many results. Additionally, we view the Beyerer and Geisler Framework as part of security economics.

1 Introduction

When faced with the task to build or improve a system in terms of both safety and security at the same time, one has to rely as to the author's best knowledge on heuristics and intuition as there exists very little rigorous theory which can be used in practice. Moreover, we can see that there are serious logical limitations in achieving safety and security. Take for example the problem of a virus scanner on a computer. Then perfectly detecting whether a program is either malicious or safe to execute is impossible as this would solve the halting problem (see for example [Coh87]). For the same reason it is impossible to decide in general whether a program will crash or not. This of course does not imply that we cannot improve the safety and security of a computer such that it will be good enough in practice. Another theoretical problem is the uncertainty of the NP=P-Problem, as for example elliptic curve cryptography relies on the problem that factoring in the associated group is a computational hard problem, which would brake down if NP=P would be true (with a reasonable value). Again this does not mean that we should consider cryptography as unsafe. But it implies that we have to constantly question our belief about the effectiveness of the cryptography used and its implementations.

Some security or safety incidents easily lead to monetary loss. The easiest case is just some amount of stolen money. In many cases likely-hood of a security or safety incident is quite rare, but in (not exclusively) financial terms the incident could be catastrophic (e. g. fire, flood-damage, full-loss of data). Further, often a similar risk for such incidents is shared by many players. In such cases, they could form a group and pay for each other's damages. In case the group is large enough and the risk of each player is independent, then by the law of large numbers they should only pay roughly the same amount every year. Of course in reality this is done via buying an insurance (if there is one available for the specific problem). Of course in some cases such as the loss of data or in case of stolen personal information of customers the true damage is much harder to quantify and it can be much more case specific. Also, note that there can be a significant difference in the damage done to the subject and what an attacker can gain. Think for example about a blown up automatic teller machine, where on top of the monetary loss, there are also the costs of repair. Even if there is no damage beyond the stolen item, there can still be a big gap. Take for example a famous painting, which is if stolen almost impossible to sell and hence is likely to have a far smaller monetary value for the thief. A more rigorous type cost analysis for cybercrimes can be found in [ABB+13]. The paper [Her12] is investigating this type of question by asking *Why Do Nigerian Scammers Say They are From Nigeria?*.

Furthermore, this type of economic analysis has been already heavily studied in the area of internet security. As a starting point for this, see for example the survey [MA11] or the website[Uni] of Ross Anderson. In the paper [And01] the hardness of information security is evaluated; It is concluded that information security is more than the technical problem alone, many problems can be better explained with the ideas of microeconomics such as *network externalities, asymmetric information, moral hazard, adverse selection, liability dumping and the tragedy of the commons.*

2 Summary of Beyerer and Geisler's Framework

We give a short summary of the relevant aspects of the framework for modelling safety and security introduced in [BG16]. The general idea is that there are several agents, each of them belongs to a certain role, which is either a *sources of danger*, subjects with flanks of vulnerabilities or protectors. The subjects are denoted by a set S and the set of vulnerabilities of a subject $s \in S$ are denoted as F_s. Part of *sources of dangers*, which is denoted as D, is purely stochastical, i. e. it resembles random events. The other agents have subjective views about the world and update their beliefs according to Bayes' theorem. More precisely, D splits up into wilful danger D_{w}, i. e. the attacker acts intentionally and intelligently to maximise their utility, and into unintended danger D_{U}, i. e. the result of random events. Further, D_{W} splits up into D_{WP} where the attacker wants to achieve a purpose[1] and into D_{WM} where the attacks follow only the purpose of the attack itself[2]. The source of unintended danger D_{U} splits up into D_{UC} which is the danger coming from carelessness or negligence[3] and D_{UR} purely random events[4].

3 Strategic game

In this section, we will now translate the Framework of Beyerer and Geisler to the language of game theory.

Definition 1. *A **game** is a tuple $G = (A_p, u_p)_{1 \leq p \leq N}$ where $\{1, \ldots, N\}$ is the set of players*[5]*, A_p is the set of action of player p and $u_p : A \to \mathbb{R}$ is the utility function of player p (i. e. the payoff) where $A := \prod_{p=1}^{N} A_p$.*

[1] e. g. copy data, steal money or goods etc.
[2] e. g. vandalism
[3] e. g. inattention, breach of duties
[4] e. g. natural disasters, technical failure etc.
[5] In Beyerer2016 this are the agents

We have 5 different types of players $D_{\text{WP}}, D_{\text{WM}}, D_{\text{UC}}, D_{\text{UR}}, P$. We let the action space of each player of the game is a subset of the Cartesian product of the union of all flanks of vulnerability of each subject, i. e. $\bigcup_{s\in S} F_s$ and a subset of the union of the following; A be the space of all attacks, I be the space of all incidents and M be the space of all measures (of defence).

3.1 Action space

Each player $d \in D_{\text{W}}$ has an action space $A_d \subset \bigcup_{s\in S} F_s \times A$ (which can change over time, and he can take according to his budget $b_d(t)$). Each player $d \in D_{\text{UC}} \cup D_{\text{UR}}$ has an action space $I_d \subset \bigcup_{s\in S} F_s \times I$. The players of D_{U} play their actions at random, but for a player $d \in D_{\text{UC}}$ we assume that the probability of causing an incident (i, f) is negatively correlated to $\int_0^1 k(i, f, \beta)d\beta$ where $k(i, f, \beta)$ are the cost of d for causing an incident i on flank f with success β. A protector player $p \in P$ has an action space M_p. His goal is to minimise the threats to some subjects $S_p \subset S$ and hence $M_p \subset \bigcup_{s\in S_p} F_s \times M$. We let M_p^* be the action taken by p.

3.2 Utility functions

The utility of a player $d \in D_{\text{W}}$ for an action (a, f) with success $0 \leq \beta \leq 1$ is

$$c_{\text{effort}}(a, f) + (c_{\text{penalty}}(a, f) \Pr(\text{penalty}|a, f\beta) + g(f, \beta)).$$

We denote this utility as $u_d(\bigcup_{p\in P} M_p^*, a, f, \beta)$. Further, let $p(\beta| \bigcup_{p\in P} M_p^*, a, f)$ be the probability density of success β when executing action (a, f) while the protector players choose $\bigcup_{p\in P} M_p^*$ as their action. The idea here is that the application of a measure will decrease the probability of success of some attack or incident on some flanks. Now we let

$$\int u_d(\bigcup_{p\in P} M_p^*, a, f, \beta)p(\beta| \bigcup_{p\in P} M_p^*, a, f)d\beta$$

be the definition of the utility of the player for the action (a, f).

An action $m(f) \in M_p$ costs the player $c(m(f))$.[6] But applying similar measures to different subjects potentially reduces cost per measure (economies of scale).[7] The overall actions he can take are according to the budget given, i.e. $b(p)$. Applying the measures M_p^* will cost the protector $\sum_{m \in M_p^*} c(m(f))$. The protector's utility density function $u_p(a, f, \beta)$ for any attack or incident a with success β on flank f is

$$c(f, \beta)p(\beta | \bigcup_{p \in P} M_p^* a, f)$$

And hence the utility for the protector for an attack or incident a on flank f

$$\int_0^1 u_d(a, f, \beta)p(\beta | \bigcup_{p \in P} M_p^*, a, f)d\beta.$$

Now we are finished with our definition of the game. Each player now has an action space and a utility function which is interdependent on the actions the other players choose. We can now start reasoning about this model by applying game theoretic results. So we can conclude, if we assume that the utility function is continuous (or each player has only finitely many actions) and the action spaces are compact metric spaces, that then the game has a Nash equilibrium. If we are in doubt whether our agents will behave fully-rational, we could use other strategies as suggested in [WLB17].

What we have not dealt with is the issue that the success of an attack depends on the success of other attacks or incidents of players. Take for example the hostile takeover of a computer for the purpose of bitcoin mining, now if another attacker has also access to the very same computer and also uses it for bitcoin mining then the expected gain should only be less than half of what would be otherwise expected. Even worse if some thunderstorm destroys the computer, before any bitcoins can flow, then the gains should be zero.

---

[6] Note that a measure costs can change over time, such as some measures have a large initial cost but then cost almost nothing (e. g. a fence).

[7] For example, developing some piece of security software costs some fixed amount, but the price of a copy is negligible.

3.2.1 Example

A producer of security measures wants to decide whether he should develop some security measure m. He estimates the fix costs at c_m and the cost per measure applied as c_a. Now he wants to know whether he can sell enough measures (let S be the set of all tuples (m, x) measures sold for x) for a good enough price such that

$$c_d + \sum_{(m,x)\in S} c_a(m) + \sum_{(m,x)\in S} x \geq 0. \tag{3.1}$$

For that we have to determine, if there exists new games where measure m is available for to all the protectors P for a certain price x, enough protectors are going to apply the measure m for their price such that Equation (3.1) is full-filled. Note that the price of the producer is not necessarily the price of the protector. Take for example a big fence with some barbed wire, it may not be allowed to install (so we may assume that the costs for the protector would be infinite). Or the protector has to stop the production line of his company in order to install the measure, which will then of course result in additional costs.

4 Bayesian game

We extend the above game to follow the rules of Bayesian game. As in the above game, it is assumed that all the players will have full knowledge about their own and the others players' action spaces and utility functions. In a Bayesian game on the other hand, the player have only incomplete information available, but have beliefs about the action spaces and utility functions of the other players. So lets first formally define what a Bayesian game is.

Definition 2. *A* ***Bayesian game*** *is a tuple* $\Gamma = ((T_i, \mathcal{T}_i), A_i, u_i, p)_{1\leq i\leq N}$ *with* $A := \prod_{i=1}^N A_i$ *and* $T := \prod_{i=1}^N T_i$ *where*

- $\{1, \ldots, N\}$ *is the set of players;*
- $(T_i, \mathcal{T}_i)$ *is a measurable space*[8], *where* T_i *is the* i*'s non-empty type space. Further we let* $\mathcal{T} = \otimes_{i=1}^N \mathcal{T}_i$;[9]

[8] Note that, if T_i is discrete, then we may ignore $\mathcal{T}_i$, as in this case it is the power set.

[9] The product σ-algebra.

- *A_i is the space of actions of player i, a non-empty metric space*[10]
- *$u_i : T \times A \to \mathbb{R}$ is i's bounded utility function, which is measurable by the σ-algebra $\left(\mathcal{T} \otimes [\otimes_{i=1}^{N} \mathcal{B}(A_i)], \mathcal{B}(\mathbb{R})\right)$;*
- *p is a probability measure on $(T, \mathcal{T})$ which denotes the common prior over the type profiles.*

Now if we want to model the Beyerer-Geisler framework as a Bayesian game we need to define the type space T. The type space T_p for player p in P consist of tuple of functions which map the objective costs and objective probabilities to the player's subjective view. So it consists of functions $\nu_{p,c(m)}$ which maps the objective cost of some measure m (on flank f of subject s) to the subjective cost of p. Also, some function ν_p which maps $c(f, \beta)$ to the subjective cost of p. Then some function π_p which maps the probabilities $p(\beta | \bigcup_{j \in P} M_j^*, i, f)$,$\Pr(i | \bigcup_{j \in P} M_j^*, f)$ $p(\beta | \bigcup_{j \in P} M_j^*, a, s, f)$ and $\Pr(a | \bigcup_{j \in P} M_j^*, s, f)$ to those subjectively assumed by p. We may also assume that the player p does only know his type up to some probability measure X_p on T_p Together this leads to some new subjective utility function $R_{p, \bigcup_{p \in P} M_p^*}(\nu_{p,c(m)}, \nu_p, \pi_p)$.

The type space for player d in D_W consists of a map $\nu_{d,c(a)}$ which maps the objective costs $c_{\text{effort}}(a, s, f)$, $(c_{\text{penalty}}(a, s, f)$ and $g(s, f, \beta))$ to the subjective costs of d. Also, there is a function π_d which maps $\Pr(\text{penalty} | a, s, f, \beta)$ and $p(\beta | a, s, f)$. to the subjective probabilities assumed by d. Again we may assume that the player d only knows his type up to some probability measure X_i.

Having set up the framework of Beyerer and Geisler like this we can apply the results of [CNM14] and know that the game (under some minor continuity assumptions or in the discrete case) has a Bayes-Nash-equilibrium.

5 Introducing temporal dynamics

We introduce some temporal dynamics now. So assume that the finite time horizon is given by $\mathfrak{T} = \{0, 1, \ldots, k\}$. Now the state of the system has three components

[10] If A_i is finite, we may assume that it is a set without any additional structure.

at time i: The type space $(T_i, \mathcal{T}_i)$, the common knowledge (prior) $\mathfrak{p}_i$ and the private assumptions $X_i^p = (\nu^i_{p,c(m)}, \nu^i_p, \pi^i_p)$ of player p. We denote the action space at time i of each player p A_i^p. Note that the action space of an protector player depends on $b_p(t)$. We may also assume that rather than having a new budget every round a protector player has fixed amount of money for some fixed number of rounds, say $t_{k'}$. So the action a player can take depends on the actions already taken.

For a player in $d \in D_W$, the actions the player can take are again limited by his budget $b_d(t)$ plus sometimes he can reinvest the eventual gains. Again he may assume that d has some fixed amount of money for some fixed number of rounds, say $t_{k'}$. So the action a player can take depends on the actions already taken.

So in this case if the subjective assumption of the players match the private assumptions, hence if our model is a non-Bayesian game, we can think of this temporal dynamic as an extensive-form game. When the game is finite, we can think of such a game in terms of a game tree. This game has again Nash-equilibria, but in this context they can be unrealistic. A solution to this problem are subgame perfect equilibria, which compared to ordinary Nash-equilibria have the additional property, that they are also equilibria for every subgame. Their existence can be shown via backward induction.

In terms of the Bayesian game model, we can go over to sequential Bayesian game. Again the concept of Bayes-Nash-equilibrium leads to unrealistic equilibria, but in case our game is finite, we can show the existence of perfect Bayesian equilibria which overcome this issue.

Another idea would be to use the framework of [OTT17]. This framework assumes that the common knowledge evolves as

$$P_{i+1} = f_i(P_i, A_i, W_i^C),$$

where f_i is function of common knowledge and W_i^C is a random variable which represents the randomness of the evolution. Then we assume that a player observes

$$Y_i^p = l_i^p(X_i^p, A_i, W_i^p),$$

where W_i^C is again a random variable which represents some random noise. We further assume that f_i^p is common knowledge among all players.[11] There are no

[11] This just means that if the players would swap their positions they would observe the same.

hard general results for this type of framework, but it is at least suspected that there exist equilibria solutions for this framework in general.

6 Conclusion and future work

We redefined the framework of Beyerer and Geisler in terms of game theory. This opens access to a deep theory for example the existence of the Nash equilibria. This immediately raises the question on the suboptimalities of these stability points of the game in terms of the social optimum (cf. [GCC08]). Moreover, many other results of game theory seem to be relevant as well, such as the study of how humans behave in these kind of strategical interactions. What also can be seen is that the task of the protector player can be a very hard problem. Not only do they have to think about their own flanks of vulnerabilities, but they also have to get a good idea of the adversary's capabilities and their motivation, e. g. their utility function.

We raise the question whether we can improve our predicting abilities of different security polices. Take for example the choice of password polices. Could we have predicted that the policies of forcing to change the passwords regularly will lead to questionable security (cf. [ZMR10]). Another question we can ask is the model's ability to predict what happens for the problem, when the protector does not have to bear the cost of failure. This is for example the case for proprietary software, the protector is the copy-right holder but the one who will suffer first is the user (cf. [MA11]).

This leads to the question of how the model we defined can be used apart for a purely theoretical quality analysis. One idea we want to investigate in the future is the question whether multi-agent simulations with our model in mind will lead to good predictions in terms of security engineering but also in terms of what political decisions such as the European General Data Protection Regulation will achieve for the personal data protection of its citizens.

Bibliography

[ABB+13] Ross Anderson, Chris Barton, Rainer Böhme, Richard Clayton, Michel JG Van Eeten, Michael Levi, Tyler Moore, and Stefan Savage. Measuring the cost of cybercrime. In *The economics of information security and privacy*, pages 265–300. Springer, 2013.

[And01] Ross Anderson. Why information security is hard-an economic perspective. In *Computer security applications conference, 2001. acsac 2001. proceedings 17th annual*, pages 358–365. IEEE, 2001.

[BG16] Jürgen Beyerer and Jürgen Geisler. A framework for a uniform quantitative description of risk with respect to safety and security. *European Journal for Security Research*, 1(2):135–150, 10 2016.

[CNM14] Oriol Carbonell-Nicolau and Richard McLean. On the existence of nash equilibrium in bayesian games. Departmental working papers, Rutgers University, Department of Economics, 2014.

[Coh87] Fred Cohen. Computer viruses. *Comput. Secur.*, 6(1):22–35, February 1987.

[GCC08] Jens Grossklags, Nicolas Christin, and John Chuang. Secure or insure?: a game-theoretic analysis of information security games. In *Proceedings of the 17th international conference on World Wide Web*, pages 209–218. ACM, 2008.

[Her12] Cormac Herley. Why do nigerian scammers say they are from nigeria? *WEIS*, June 2012.

[MA11] Tyler Moore and Ross Anderson. Economics and internet security: A survey of recent analytical, empirical, and behavioral research. 2011.

[OTT17] Yi Ouyang, Hamidreza Tavafoghi, and Demosthenis Teneketzis. Dynamic games with asymmetric information: Common information based perfect bayesian equilibria and sequential decomposition. *IEEE Transactions on Automatic Control*, 62(1):222–237, 2017.

[Uni] Ross Anderson Cambridge University.

[WLB17] James R Wright and Kevin Leyton-Brown. Predicting human behavior in unrepeated, simultaneous-move games. *Games and Economic Behavior*, 106:16–37, 2017.

[ZMR10] Yinqian Zhang, Fabian Monrose, and Michael K Reiter. The security of modern password expiration: An algorithmic framework and empirical analysis. In *Proceedings of the 17th ACM conference on Computer and communications security*, pages 176–186. ACM, 2010.

Supervised Laplacian Eigenmaps for Hyperspectral Data

Florian Becker

Vision and Fusion Laboratory
Institute for Anthropomatics
Karlsruhe Institute of Technology (KIT), Germany
florian.becker@kit.edu

Technical Report IES-2018-09

Abstract

With Laplacian eigenmaps the low-dimensional manifold of high-dimensional data points can be uncovered. This nonlinear dimensionality reduction technique is popular due to its well-understood theoretical foundation. This paper outlines a straightforward way to incorporate class label information into the standard (unsupervised) Laplacian eigenmaps formulation. With the example of hyperspectral data samples this supervised reformulation is shown to reinforce within-class clustering and increase between-class distances.

1 Introduction

Advances in hyperspectral image acquisition and domain-specific machine learning methods for clustering and classification of the acquired data are progressing in tandem. By its very nature hyperspectral images tend to be high-dimensional as sensors capture many narrow and contiguous spectral bands and algorithms for analysis often combine spatial as well as spectral information. Due to the high resolution of many hyperspectral image (HSI) data sets, it has been suggested to employ nonlinear dimensionality reduction (or *manifold learning*) as a method to embed high dimensional data points in a lower dimensional space, while preserving the local geometry. Nonlinear dimensionality reduction has proven itself useful in many different domains, like face recognition [CK09], speech recognition [BO95] and image retrieval [LLC05]. In contrast to a principal component analysis, where data points are projected onto a linear subspace, nonlinear dimensionality reduction techniques can find the low-dimensional nonlinear manifold that is possibly embedded inside a higher-dimensional space. Manifold learning is therefore very suitable for data sets, where an intrinsic low-dimensional structure is suspected. A classical example of this is an image series of a person looking in various different directions. The images itself are rather high-dimensional, the intrinsic lower dimension however, can be characterized by a Euclidean space, where one axis represents looking right and left, and the other axis up and down [RYS04]. Manifold learning methods are generally able to find this structure. In this paper, we focus on Laplacian eigenmaps (LE), a classical manifold learning algorithm [BN03]. We show how the standard LE formulation can be adapted in order to take class labels into account and how this supervised reformulation is an improvement.

Different approaches to incorporate class label information into manifold learning applications have already been considered. In [RD12] for instance, one within-class and one between-class graph was constructed to achieve a supervised manifold learning formulation. In contrast to this, we show that one graph and the associated affinity matrix equipped with a certain kernel function is sufficient.

The remainder of this technical report is organized as follows: We first begin by revisiting the standard Laplacian eigenmaps formulation and motivate the importance of the Laplacian matrix and its relation to the Laplace operator. In the following section the supervised version of the Laplacian eigenmaps method is outlined. The algorithm is evaluated by using a hyperspectral dataset that was acquired by the AVIRIS sensor. We show quantitative and qualitative results.

2 Laplacian Eigenmaps

Given data samples $\mathcal{X} = \{\mathbf{x}_i\}_{i=0}^{n} \subseteq \mathbb{R}^m$ many classical manifold learning algorithms start with the construction of an undirected weighted graph $G = (V, W)$, where each node $v_j \in V$ represents one data point and W is the $n \times n$ affinity matrix. Affinity or similarity can intuitively be understood as an inverse distance measure.[1] Note, that the dimensionality m of the data points does not appear in W, as it encodes all pairwise affinities. One common affinity measure is the so called Gaussian heat kernel

$$W_{ij} = k_{\text{Gauss}}(\mathbf{x}_i, \mathbf{x}_j; \beta) = e^{\frac{-||x_i - \mathbf{x}_j||_2^2}{\beta}},$$

with $\beta \in \mathbb{R}$. This Gaussian heat kernel is applied to all $\mathbf{x}_j, \mathbf{x}_k \in \mathcal{X}$, provided that the Euclidean distance between the samples is smaller than a certain $\varepsilon > 0$. In general, we call a symmetric function $k : \mathcal{X} \times \mathcal{X} \to \mathbb{R}$ a kernel, if the induced *Gram matrix* defined by $K_{ij} = k(\mathbf{x_i}, \mathbf{x_j})$ is positive semi-definite. Choosing an adequate affinity measure is of course one crucial aspect of LE. When dealing with signals or (hyper)spectral data, one might for instance consider the cosine similarity or dynamic time warping. For the time being, we focus on the Gaussian heat kernel. After the construction of the weighted graph G, the *eigenmaps*, which define the mapping to the low-dimensional space, must be computed. Therefore, the generalized eigenvector problem must be solved:

$$L\mathbf{y} = \lambda D\mathbf{y}, \tag{2.1}$$

where $L = D - W$ is the so called Laplacian matrix, and D the diagonal degree matrix.

Now, if $\mathbf{y}_0, \ldots, \mathbf{y}_{n-1}$ are the solutions to the above generalized eigenvalue equation (2.1), then order the equations according to the eigenvalues, such that λ_0 is the smallest:

$$\begin{aligned} L\mathbf{y}_0 &= \lambda_0 D\mathbf{y}_0 \\ L\mathbf{y}_1 &= \lambda_1 D\mathbf{y}_1 \\ &\vdots \\ L\mathbf{y}_{n-1} &= \lambda_{n-1} D\mathbf{y}_{n-1} \end{aligned}$$

[1] Note however, that affinity measures are not necessarily required to be an inverse metric. For instance, the inverse of the dynamic time warping distance could be used as an affinity measure (see e.g. [SNNS02]), although it is only a *semi*-metric, i.e. it does not satisfy the triangle inequality.

Finally, the mapping $\Phi : \mathbb{R}^m \to \mathbb{R}^p$ into a p-dimensional target space is defined by the p eigenvectors:

$$\Phi(\mathbf{x}_i) = [\,\mathbf{y}_1(i), \ldots, \mathbf{y}_p(i)\,]^T$$

The goal is to have a mapping, where $\mathbf{y}_i$ and $\mathbf{y}_j$ are "close" together, i.e. we want to minimize

$$\begin{aligned}\sum_{ij}(\mathbf{y}_i - \mathbf{y}_j)^2 W_{ij} &= \sum_{ij}(\mathbf{y}_i^2 + \mathbf{y}_j^2 - 2\mathbf{y}_i\mathbf{y}_j)W_{ij} \\ &= \sum_i \mathbf{y}_i^2 D_{ii} + \sum_j \mathbf{y}_j^2 D_{jj} - 2\sum_{ij} \mathbf{y}_i\mathbf{y}_j W_{ij} \\ &= 2\mathbf{y}^T L\mathbf{y}.\end{aligned}$$

The last step of the above derivation is true because by definition $D_{ii} = \sum_j W_{ji}$. Hence, the minimization problem reduces to

$$\underset{\mathbf{y}^T D\mathbf{y}=1}{\operatorname{argmin}}\ \mathbf{y}^T L\mathbf{y}.$$

Finding a vector $\mathbf{y}$ that minimizes this objective function is equivalent in finding the eigenvectors of Equation (2.1).

3 Laplace Operator

The Laplacian matrix plays an important role in graph theory and can for instance be used to approximate the sparsest cut of a graph [AHK10] or to compute s-t flows [CKM$^+$11]. Another interesting property of the Laplacian matrix is that it can be understood as an discrete Laplace operator. In this subsection, we will motivate this aspect of the Laplacian matrix. To begin with, consider the definition of the Laplace operator, which is a second order differential operator of a function ϕ:

$$\Delta\phi = \sum_{i=1}^{n} \frac{\partial^2 \phi}{\partial x_i^2},$$

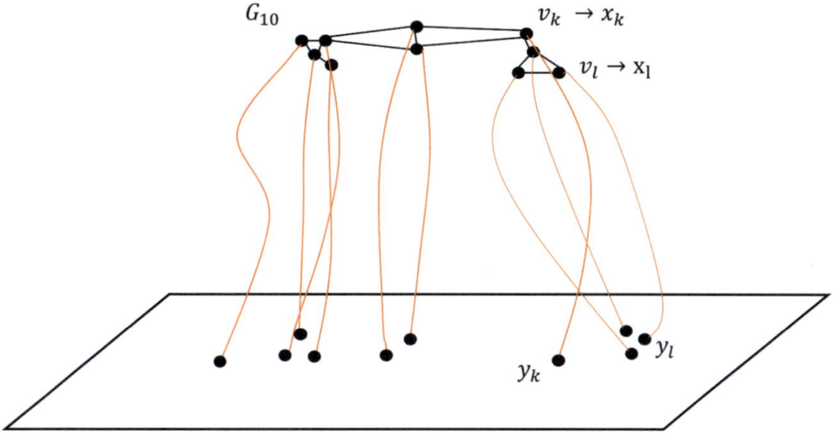

Figure 2.1: Conceptual projection of a data set with ten samples. Every of the vertices of G_{10} stands for one such data point. With $v_k \to x_k$ we denote that x_k is "represented" by v_k. The length of the edges is according to a certain affinity/kernel function, i.e. shorter edges mean a higher affinity. This must be reflected by the projection: A high affinity between nodes must lead to the points being "close" together in the lower-dimensional space.

where ϕ is a twice-differentiable function. $\Delta\phi$ is called the *Laplacian* of ϕ. Now, as we want to relate this continuous Laplace operator to the analogous discrete case, consider a grid, or rather any arbitrary undirected weighted graph G and let $\psi : V \to \mathbb{R}$ be a function that maps every node v_j of G to a real number $\nu_j = \psi(v_j)$. For the sake of vividness, assume that this number represents a temperature ν_j^t at a discrete time step t. The following derivation relates the temperature change $\Delta^{t:t+1}\nu_i = ||\nu_i^t - \nu_i^{t+1}||$ from time step t to $t+1$ to the difference of the neighboring nodes temperatures, where W_{ij} can be thought of as the heat conduction between nodes v_j and v_i.

$$\Delta^{t:t+1}\nu_i \propto -\sum_j W_{ij}(\nu_i - \nu_j)$$

$$
\begin{aligned}
&= -(\nu_i \sum_j W_{ij} - \sum_j W_{ij}\nu_j) \\
&= -(\nu_i \deg_W(v_i) - \sum_j W_{ij}\nu_j) \\
&= -\sum_j (\delta_{ij} \deg_W(v_i) - W_{ij})\nu_j \\
&= -\sum_j L_{ij}\nu_j
\end{aligned}
$$

$\deg_W(v_i)$ denotes i-th row (or column)[2] sum of W and δ_{ij} is the Kronecker delta.

We see that from the simple fact that the change in temperature is proportional to the difference of the neighboring temperatures (*Newton's law of cooling*), the Laplacian matrix L emerges. The above derivation of heat transfer on a graph resembles the heat equation

$$
\frac{\partial u}{\partial t} = -\alpha \Delta u,
$$

where the Laplacian matrix replaces the Laplace operator.

Consider the weighted graph from Figure 3.1 and its corresponding weight matrix W, diagonal degree matrix D and the resulting Laplacian matrix L. Multiplying the vector of node numbers with the Laplacian matrix, gives the negative change of those node temperatures for the next time-step.

4 Supervised Laplacian Eigenmaps

In order to incorporate class label information, we construct the affinity matrix as follows. Let $(\mathbf{x}_i, \ell) \in \mathbb{R}^m \times \{1, \ldots, L\}$ or $\mathbf{x}_i^\ell$ for short be a data sample and its associated label in a multi-class setting. The entries of $W \in (0, 1]^{n \times n}$ are then computed as:

[2] Since W is symmetric, row and column sums are equal.

$$W_{i,j} := \begin{cases} \sqrt{k_{Gauss}(\mathbf{x}_i^\ell, \mathbf{x}_j^o; \beta)} & \text{if } \ell = o \\ \gamma \, k_{Gauss}(\mathbf{x}_i^\ell, \mathbf{x}_j^o; \beta) & \text{if } \ell \neq o, \end{cases} \tag{4.1}$$

where β is set to the average pairwise Euclidean distance of all $\{\mathbf{x}_i\}_{i=0}^n \subseteq \mathbb{R}^m$.

Speaking in terms of an heat distribution over the nodes, we want to inhibit the heat flow between two nodes if they do not have the same label. This is simply realized by the parameter $\gamma \in (0, 1)$ in Eq. (4.1). This *inhibition* parameter is a straightforward way to influence the affinity measure. Setting $\gamma = \varepsilon$ for $\varepsilon > 0$ will have the effect of increasing between-class distances in the target space, while $\gamma = 1 - \varepsilon$ will converge to the standard LE result.

However, similar data points should be close together on the projected space independent of their class, which is why the kernel function k is used in both cases. By this approach, both desired goals are achieved: First, samples sharing the same label are reinforced to fall into the same region. Second, data points with different labels are repelled from each other by a certain factor, but nevertheless their overall closeness is still defined by the inhibited but otherwise same kernel function.

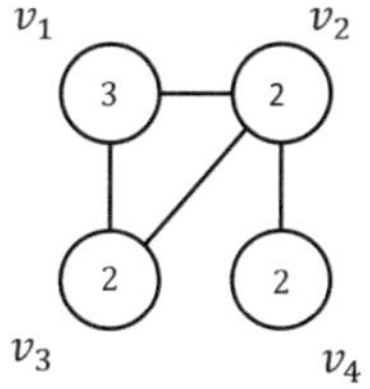

$$\begin{bmatrix} 0.8 & 0 & 0 & 0 \\ 0 & 2.5 & 0 & 0 \\ 0 & 0 & 1.7 & 0 \\ 0 & 0 & 0 & 1 \end{bmatrix} - \begin{bmatrix} 0 & 0.3 & 0.5 & 0 \\ 0.3 & 0 & 1.2 & 1 \\ 0.5 & 1.2 & 0 & 0 \\ 0 & 1 & 0 & 0 \end{bmatrix} = \begin{bmatrix} 0.8 & -0.3 & -0.5 & 0 \\ -0.3 & 2.5 & -1.2 & -1 \\ -0.5 & -1.2 & 0 & 0 \\ 0 & -1 & 0 & 1 \end{bmatrix}$$

Figure 3.1: A weighted undirected graph with $\boldsymbol{\nu} = [\psi(v_1), \psi(v_2), \psi(v_3), \psi(v_3)] = [3, 2, 2, 2]^T$, the corresponding diagonal degree matrix, weight matrix and Laplacian matrix. Multiplying $\boldsymbol{\nu}$ with the Laplacian matrix results in the negative change from one time step to another: $L\boldsymbol{\nu} = [0.8, -0.3, -0.5, 0.0]^T$.

4.1 Experiments & Results

We evaluate the performance of the proposed supervised Laplacian eigenmaps procedure using the k-nearest neighbor method. Independent of supervised or unsupervised, the expectation of different manifold learning algorithms is that similar data samples must be located close to each other in the projected low-dimensional space, given any suitable, i.e. domain-specific, distance function. Therefore, a reasonable approach is to inspect every data point and look for the label of its 1-nearest neighbor. For the evaluation of the proposed supervised Laplacian eigenmaps method, we use spectral information that was acquired by the AVIRIS sensor at the *Indian Pines* test site in Indiana–a standard dataset, that is commonly used in remote sensing research. There are all in all 16 different classes; two-thirds of the scene are composed of agriculture (corn, oats, soybean, wheat, etc.), one-thirds of forest.

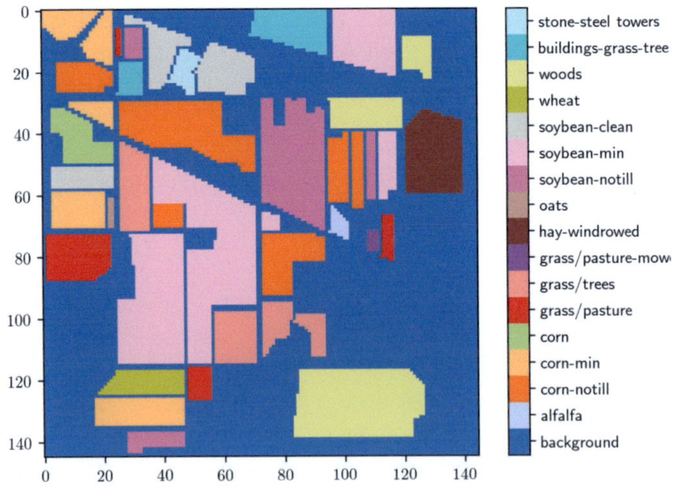

Figure 4.1: Indian pines acquired by the NASA AVIRIS sensor. The same color coding for the classes is also used for Figure 4.2.

The embedding in a low-dimensional target space depends very much of γ. Figure 4.2 depicts the embedding into the Euclidean space for two different values of $\gamma \in \{0.25, 0.75\}$ and also the standard embedding by LE. For $\gamma = 0.25$ some clusters are widely separated from each other, while for $\gamma = 0.75$ clusters are generally closer together.

All in all there are 200 spectral reflectance bands in the range of 400nm to 2500nm. As the data set consists of over twenty thousand hyperspectral pixels, it is computationally infeasible to solve the generalized eigenvalue decomposition as its complexity is $\mathcal{O}(n^3)$. Therefore, we subsample the data set, apply our method repeatedly to smaller chunks of the data and average the performance to get an overall score. We test this procedure for different values of $\gamma \in \{0.1, 0.2, \ldots, 0.9\}$.

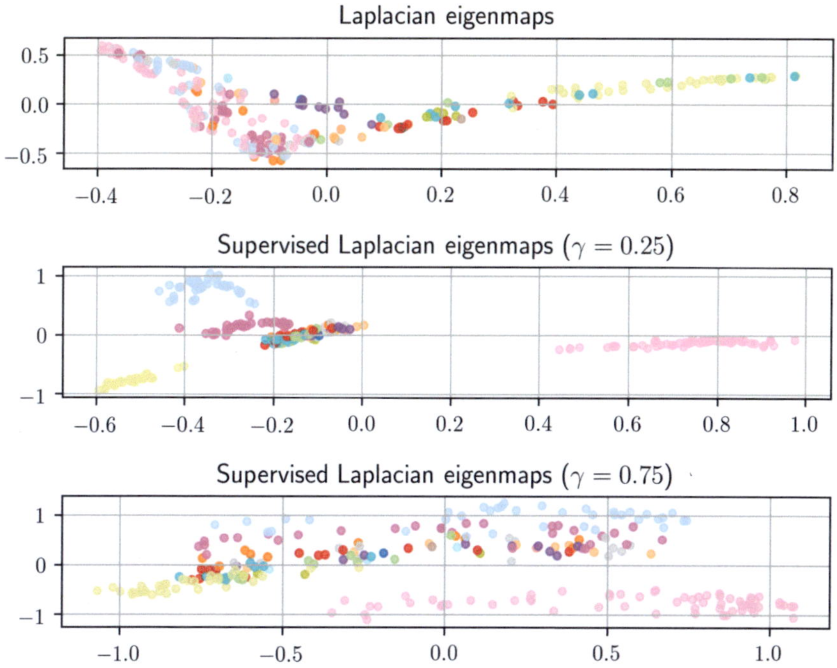

Figure 4.2: Qualitative results: 200-dimensional spectral data points are projected onto the Euclidean plane. It can be seen that in all cases spectra with the same label cluster together. However, when class label information is used in the construction of the weight matrix, same-label clusters are denser and different-label clusters are further apart. This effect is reinforced when using a small γ.

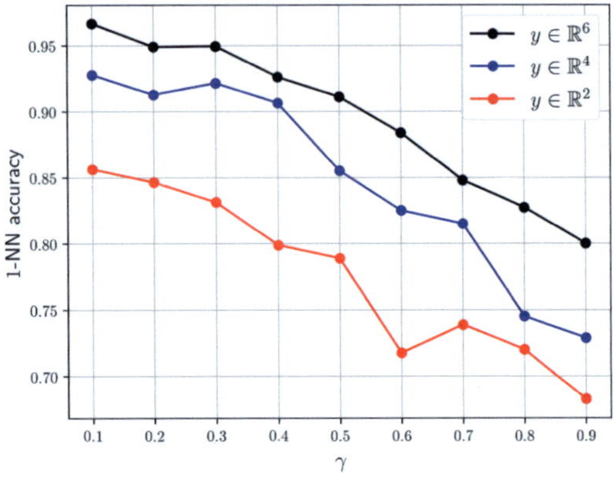

Figure 4.3: 1-nearest neighbor accuracy for different values of γ and target dimensions $\mathbb{R}^2$, $\mathbb{R}^4$ and $\mathbb{R}^6$.

Figure 4.3 shows the 1-nearest neighbor accuracy for different values of γ as well as for three different target dimensions. It is not surprising that a higher target dimension allows for a better performance. Note furthermore that γ has a large impact on the accuracy; decreasing the affinity between different-label data samples seems to ensure that the variance between the classes is larger than within.

5 Conclusion & Outlook

Nonlinear dimensionality reduction is a powerful tool for high-dimensional data analysis and visualization. We have shown an easy way to integrate class labels into the standard Laplacian eigenmaps formulation. By this it is possible to embed high-dimensional data into a low-dimensional space, while enhancing the within-class relations and extending the between-class distances.

Besides applying this method to other (hyperspectral) data sets, future work could include a way to parameterize γ and evaluate other procedures to build the affinity matrix. In this technical report, γ was used in order to decrease between-class affinity. Further research should investigate the impact of choosing γ according to the overall between-class dissimilarity of two different classes. This could be computed using a the very same kernel function that is used to compute the affinity matrix. An important question in general is how to choose or design a kernel function k. In this technical report, we only considered the standard heat kernel. However, other affinity measures might be more suitable for spectral data. As future steps, we plan to evaluate the performance of various different kernel functions.

Bibliography

[AHK10] Sanjeev Arora, Elad Hazan, and Satyen Kale. $O(\sqrt(logn))$ approximation to sparsest cut in $O(n^2)$ time. *SIAM Journal on Computing*, 39(5):1748–1771, 2010.

[BN03] Mikhail Belkin and Partha Niyogi. Laplacian eigenmaps for dimensionality reduction and data representation. *Neural computation*, 15(6):1373–1396, 2003.

[BO95] Christoph Bregler and Stephen M Omohundro. Nonlinear manifold learning for visual speech recognition. In *iccv*, page 494. IEEE, 1995.

[CK09] Yeongjae Cheon and Daijin Kim. Natural facial expression recognition using differential-aam and manifold learning. *Pattern Recognition*, 42(7):1340–1350, 2009.

[CKM$^+$11] Paul Christiano, Jonathan A Kelner, Aleksander Madry, Daniel A Spielman, and Shang-Hua Teng. Electrical flows, laplacian systems, and faster approximation of maximum flow in undirected graphs. In *Proceedings of the forty-third annual ACM symposium on Theory of computing*, pages 273–282. ACM, 2011.

[LLC05] Yen-Yu Lin, Tyng-Luh Liu, and Hwann-Tzong Chen. Semantic manifold learning for image retrieval. In *Proceedings of the 13th annual ACM international conference on Multimedia*, pages 249–258. ACM, 2005.

[RD12] Bogdan Raducanu and Fadi Dornaika. A supervised non-linear dimensionality reduction approach for manifold learning. *Pattern Recognition*, 45(6):2432–2444, 2012.

[RYS04] Bisser Raytchev, Ikushi Yoda, and Katsuhiko Sakaue. Head pose estimation by nonlinear manifold learning. In *Pattern Recognition, 2004. ICPR 2004. Proceedings of the 17th International Conference on*, volume 4, pages 462–466. IEEE, 2004.

[SNNS02] Hiroshi Shimodaira, Ken-ichi Noma, Mitsuru Nakai, and Shigeki Sagayama. Dynamic time-alignment kernel in support vector machine. In *Advances in neural information processing systems*, pages 921–928, 2002.

Simulation-Based Evaluation of Wavelet Coefficients for Robust Analysis of Near Infrared Spectra

Julius Krause

Vision and Fusion Laboratory
Institute for Anthropomatics
Karlsruhe Institute of Technology (KIT), Germany
julius.krause@kit.edu

Technical Report IES-2018-08

Abstract

Near infrared spectroscopy is a common method for analysis of food, soil and pharmaceutical products. New developments in sensor technology, like hyperspectral camera systems and mobile spectrometers, allow broad applications of spectroscopy with devices out of specialized laboratories. Wavelet coefficients are a promising approach for the detection and estimation of spectral absorption bands. The robustness of wavelet based features against typical measuring influences and calibration errors will be analyzed in the following by using simulations.

1 Introduction

In near infrared spectra, information from the chemical and physical properties of a sample are superimposed. Therefore, methods of multivariate data analysis and machine learning are needed to link the optically measured information with the properties of the sample. In this area, computer science overlaps with chemometrics, a sub-discipline of chemistry for the evaluation of statistical data. For this reason, there is already a large number of methods for processing spectral data. However, it turns that some classical data evaluation methods are difficult to apply to current tasks, such as networks of spectral sensors. Models for the evaluation of near infrared spectra can often only be used for single sensors calibrated by complex reference analyses [Wor18, FWT$^+$02].

One of the most serious calibration errors of spectrometers is the wavelength mapping of the individual bands, e.g. due to aging processes, temperature fluctuations or tolerances in the production process. This error has a massive influence on the model accuracy. The transferability of models between sensors and the long-term stability of the models is therefore limited.

Therefore, the wavelet transformation for the detection of absorption bands has already been presented as a promising method [BPT18]. This method explicitly determines the absorption bands, more precisely the chemical parameters of the sample. This results in feature vectors which are partly invariant to multiplicative influences such as the measuring distance and particle size.

In the following, the influence of wavelength calibration and noise errors will be investigated in more detail. A classical data preprocessing method by smoothing with Savitzky-Golay filters, derivatives and normalization with *Standard Normal Variate* (SNV) is compared with the wavelet coefficient approach [RvdBE09a].

2 Signal model of the near infrared reflection

The determination of chemical parameters, such as the concentration of individual components, is based on the properties of certain absorption bands. In many examples, bandpass filters can be used for evaluation [LBF+15a, Lu04a]. However, the absorption can only be determined indirectly, because only the light reflected from the sample reaches the sensor. Scattering effects also applies to transmission measurements, which are therefore not considered separately.

First, the signal input at the spectrometer is to be described. The number of photons hitting the sensor is determined by

$$g(\lambda) := N_{\text{sensor}}(\lambda) = (1 - P_{\text{abs}}(\lambda)) \cdot P_{\text{sca}}(\lambda) \cdot N_{\text{source}}(\lambda),$$

whereby the scattering probability is determined by integrating the radiance in the solid angle of the sensor.

The so-called *Bidirectional Reflectance Distribution Function* (BRDF) [BFP12] provides a formal description of the reflection behavior. In a spectral measurement, however, the necessary angles and the BRDF of the object are usually unknown.

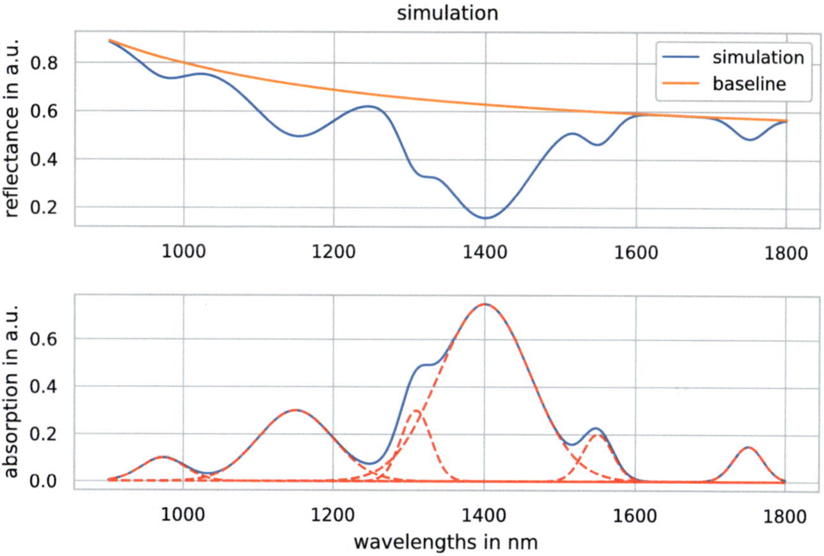

Figure 2.1: Near infrared spectra are formed from a sum of different absorptions by polar hydrogen bonds. The absorptions can be determined indirectly from the reflectance or transmission of a sample. But this signal additionally contains a wavelength dependent baseline by physical effects like Mie and Rayleigh scattering.

A theoretical description of the reflection behavior allows in parts the physical scattering theory according to Mie and Rayleigh. The result is a wavelength-dependent scattering probability that a photon is scattered into the detection range of the sensor. In order to simplify the complex scattering process, it is assumed in the following that the scattering probability is a smooth and continuously differentiable function. For this reason, the derivation in spectral direction is an established method for reducing the influence of particle size in a spectral measurement [NW84a].

The absorption probability results from

$$P_{\text{abs}}(\lambda) = \sum_{j}^{N} c_j \cdot \exp\left\{ -\left(\frac{\lambda - \lambda_j}{\sqrt{2}\sigma_j} \right)^2 \right\},$$

whereby the relationship between the expression c_j of the corresponding absorption bands and the substance concentration is well approximated by Beer-Lambert's law [Bro06a]. In many cases, constituents also act on several absorption bands, because the absorption bands are formed by excitation of molecular groups of different polar hydrogen bonds. Therefore, spectral analysis is an ill-posed non-linear inverse problem. A further complicating factor is that the absorption bands of the different molecule groups also overlap.

A spectrometer or a spectral camera forms a discrete measurement signal

$$k_i := (g * h_{i,\text{sensor}})(\lambda_i) + N_{i,\text{dark}}$$

from the incident photons. For a large number of spectral bands, depending on the system several hundred or more than thousand bands are recorded, the term *hyperspectral* is used.

In the ideal case there is no crosstalk of the bandpasses between single spectral channels

$$h_{i,\text{sensor}}(\lambda) \approx \delta(\lambda, \lambda_i + \Delta\lambda).$$

The wavelength assignment is done via the filter position λ_i, which can be shifted by $\Delta\lambda$ due to calibration errors.

The reflectance **R** of a sample is determined by comparison with an standard with ideal reflectivity

$$\begin{aligned} R_i &= \frac{k_i - k_{i,\text{dark}}}{k_{i,\text{reference}} - k_{i,\text{dark}}} \\ &= (1 - P_{\text{abs}}(\lambda_i + \Delta\lambda)) \cdot P_{\text{sca}}(\lambda_i + \Delta\lambda). \end{aligned}$$

This removes the dark current and the spectral curve of the light source. The wavelength-dependent sensitivity of the sensor, which has not been described in detail so far, is also compensated, because the detection probability of a photon is comparable to a changed number of photons from the source.

3 Wavelet feature extraction

The purpose of the feature extraction method presented here is to estimate the absorption bands contained in the spectrum. Wavelet transformation is a well-established method in image and signal processing, especially for edge detection [Mal89a] [Mor83]. Due to the similarity to P_{abs}, the analysis with the Mexican-Hat wavelet

$$\psi_{\lambda_0,s}(\lambda) = s^2 \frac{d^2}{d\lambda^2} \frac{1}{\sqrt{2\pi s}} \exp\left\{ -\left(\frac{\lambda - \lambda_0}{\sqrt{2}s} \right)^2 \right\}$$

allows a direct estimation of the absorption bands.

The Wavelet transformation

$$\Gamma_\psi^R(\lambda_0, s) := \langle \psi_{\lambda_0,s}(\lambda), R(\lambda) \rangle$$

is performed for a variety of possible positions λ_0 and scaling factors s. The absorption bands can then be determined from the positions (λ_i, s_i) of the local maxima within the wavelet scalogram. The evaluation of the wavelet coefficient $\Gamma_\psi^R(\lambda_i, s_i)$ also makes it possible to estimate the amount of absorption.

Assuming the scattering probability can be approximated as a smooth, continuously differentiable function, an approximation as a Taylor series is possible at the position of the absorption bands. This approximation allows a simplified description of scattering effects because the Mexican-Hat wavelet has two vanishing moments. Thus the influence of the scattering probability to the determination of the molecule concentration c_i is reduced to a localy static multiplicative factor

$$\begin{aligned} \Gamma_\psi^R(\lambda_i, s_i) &= \langle \psi_{\lambda_0,s}(\lambda), (1 - P_{\text{sca}}(\lambda)) P_{\text{sca}}(\lambda) \rangle \\ &\approx c_i P_{\text{sca}}(\lambda_i), \end{aligned}$$

which can be removed e.g. by quotient formation with neighbouring absorption bands. However, the position and width of the estimated absorptions are not influenced by this multiplicative factor.

4 Impact of noise and wavelength shift on prediction accuracy

Based on the signal model presented at the beginning (see fig 2.1), spectral data with different concentrations of a fictive ingredient were generated. The fictive ingredient forces linear changes of the absorption band at 1310 nm. In addition this absorption band is superimposed by a larger absorption at 1400 nm. This problem is exemplary e.g. for the determination of acid concentration by OH absorption near the water band. In addition, static absorption bands of different characteristics were added at 973 nm, 1150 nm, 1550 nm and 1700 nm (see fig 2.1). In addition, the reflectance, more precisely the baseline, was varied by a random value. For comparability all models were trained with 41 spectra, each spectrum is sampled by 300 bands between 900 nm and 1800 nm. The validation was done by newly generated spectra, which differ from the original training data by a random baseline. *Partial least squares regression* (PLSR) models with 6 components were used to compare feature extraction by wavelets with a classical spectral pre-processing.

The classical pre-processing steps are:

- a smoothing of the spectrum using Savitzky-Golay filters (11,2)
- the generation of a spectral derivative to correct the baseline
- normalizing the intensities by using *Standard Normal Variate* (SNV)

The wavelet based feature extraction was performed in the following steps:

- by use of wavelet transformation the absorption bands were determined from local maxima in Γ_ψ^R
- feature vector **m** was created with $m_i = s_i \cdot \Gamma_\psi^R(\lambda_i, s_i)$
- the feature vector **m** was normalized to the variance due to the different intensities of the spectra

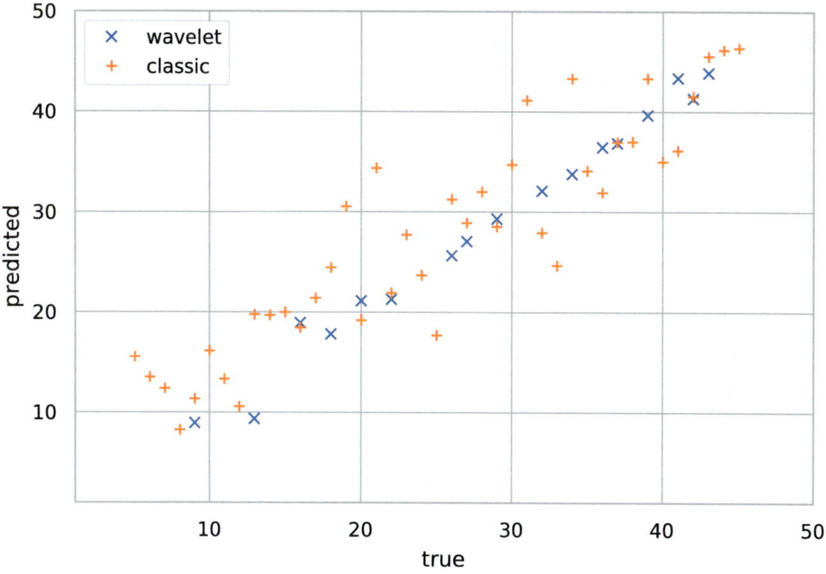

Figure 4.1: For a noise level of 0.015 of the spectral intensity, the type of prediction of both methods differs significantly. While the classical method scatters more strongly, the wavelet method, in individual cases especially at low concentrations, does not make a prediction.

4.1 Simulation of different noise levels

In real spectroscopic sensors, the measurement signal is superimposed by noise due to various processes such as discretization and amplification in signal acquisition. Therefore, the noise level of spectral bands is an important quality parameter of the sensor. A comprehensive description can be found in the EMVA1288 standard. For further evaluation, the spectral signals

$$R'_i = R_i \cdot (\text{rand}\,[\text{-}1{,}1] \cdot \text{noise level} + 1)$$

are superimposed with random noise.

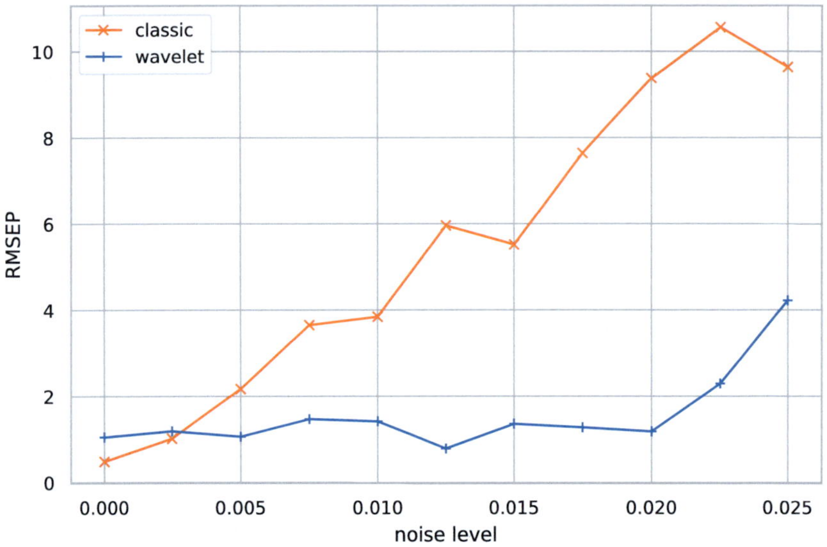

Figure 4.2: The *Root Mean Square Error of Prediction* (RMSEP) was determined for different noise levels using 41 random spectra. The wavelet method shows nearly no changes over a wide range, but this is also based on the implicit rejection of faulty spectra.

For different noise levels the *Root Mean Square Error of Prediction* (RMSEP) was determined by 41 random spectra of different concentrations 4.2. It was found that the RMSEP increased continuously with increasing noise levels when classical pre-processing was used. Using the wavelet method, the required absorption band, especially at low concentrations, was not detected with increasing noise level in some cases. Because an incorrect detection of absorption bands already leads to an error in the creation of the feature vector **m**. Therefore, the wavlet method implicitly rejects faulty data and remaining predictions lead to a better result (see fig 4.1).

4.2 Simulation of systematic wavelength shifts

As in the previous section, the two pre-processing methods were compared using systematically modified test data. The spectra were shifted step by step compared to the trained data sets.

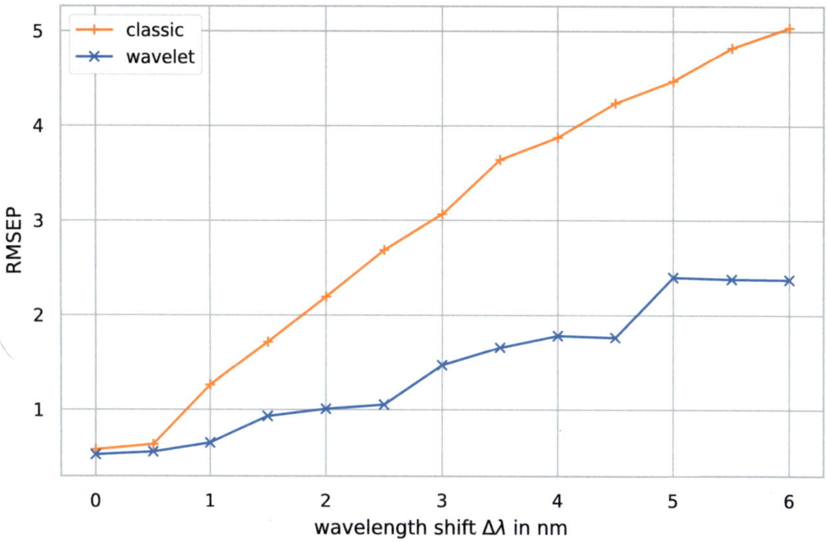

Figure 4.3: The spectra of the test dataset were shiftet systematically in wavelength compared to the training dataset. This creates a bias and therefore a continuously increasing error in prediction by the classical method. The prediction by the wavelet method changes step by step, depending on detection of the peaks within the allowed tolerance range.

Using classical preprocessing, a bias in the prediction was generated, resulting in a continuous increase of the RMSEP with increasing shift. This was to be expected in this way.

The features determined by wavelet transformation also showed a shift dependent error. However, this error is lower compared to the classical method and changes approximately stepwise. The simulation therefore evaluates the effects on the prediction error already for shifts below the spectral resolution.

5 Summary

The results of the simulations have already been expected a-priori due to the mathematical structure. The presented classical method is based on the scalar multiplication of the spectrum with a vector of coefficients, which are exactly adapted to the resolution and measurement range of the sensor. The SNV preprocessing method also uses the variance of the entire spectrum for normalization. This is the case in almost all established methods. Due to the strong adaptation to the sensor used, problems arise in the transferability of the learned models to different sensors.

The feature extraction by detection of absorption bands with a wavelet transformation uses prior knowledge about the shape of the absorption bands. This makes it possible to consider the neighborhood relationship of spectral bands. This results in a reliable detection of superimposed absorption bands and noise influences are minimized. The application of the Mexican-Hat wavelet also enables the minimization of scattering effects due to the included vanishing moments.

Especially at low concentrations, less absorption bands were detected with an increasing noise level. This correlation could be used in the future as a possibility to characterize spectral sensors. Because the signal-to-noise ratio given in the data sheets refers only to an intensity-noise-ratio of the spectral bands. Wavelets take into account the neighborhood relationship of spectral bands. Due to the limit and the uncertainty in the detection of the wavelets, a combination of resolution and noise is possible. Together with an already existing model based on wavelet features, a sensor-specific *Limt of Detection* (LoD) for certain ingredients is thinkable.

Bibliography

[BFP12] Jürgen Beyerer, Christian Frese, and Fernando Puente Leon. *Automatische Sichtprüfung : Grundlagen, Methoden und Praxis der Bildgewinnung und Bildauswertung*. Springer Vieweg, 2012.

[BPT18] Jürgen Beyerer, Alexey Pak, and Miro Taphanel, editors. *Proceedings of the 2017 Joint Workshop of Fraunhofer IOSB and Institute for Anthropomatics, Vision and Fusion Laboratory*. Karlsruher Schriften zur Anthropomatik. KIT Scientific Publishing, Karlsruhe, [2018].

[Bro06a] Adrian Jon Brown. Spectral curve fitting for automatic hyperspectral data analysis. *IEEE Transactions on Geoscience and Remote Sensing*, 44(6):1601–1607, 2006.

[FWT$^+$02] Robert N. Feudale, Nathaniel A. Woody, Huwei Tan, Anthony J. Myles, Steven D. Brown, Joan Ferre, and Joan Ferré. Transfer of multivariate calibration models: a review. *Chemometrics and Intelligent Laboratory System*, 64(2):181–12, 2002.

[LBF$^+$15a] Magali Lafontaine, Zrinka Bockaj, Maximilian Freund, Kai Uwe Vieth, Christian Negara, and Thomas Langle. Non-destructive determination of grape berry sugar concentration using visible/near infrared imaging and possible impact on wine quality. *Technisches Messen*, 2015.

[Lu04a] Renfu Lu. Multispectral imaging for predicting firmness and soluble solids content of apple fruit. *Postharvest Biology and Technology*, 31(2):147–157, 2004.

[Mal89a] S.G. Stephane G. Mallat. A Theory for Multiresolution Signal Decomposition: The Wavelet Representation. *IEEE Transactions on Pattern Analysis and Machine Intelligence*, 11(7):674–693, jul 1989.

[Mor83] J. Morlet. Sampling theory and wave propagation. In *Issues in acoustic signal/image processing and recognition*, volume 1, pages 233–261. Springer Berlin Heidelberg, Berlin, Heidelberg, 1983.

[NW84a] KH Norris and PC Williams. Optimization of mathematical treatments of raw near-infrared signal in the measurement of protein in hard red spring wheat. I. Influence of particle size., 1984.

[RvdBE09a] Åsmund Rinnan, Frans van den Berg, and Søren Balling Engelsen. Review of the most common pre-processing techniques for near-infrared spectra. *TrAC Trends in Analytical Chemistry*, 28(10):1201–1222, nov 2009.

[Wor18] Jerome J. Workman. A Review of Calibration Transfer Practices and Instrument Differences in Spectroscopy, mar 2018.

A Behaviour Model as Extension for the Object-Oriented World Model

Mathias Anneken

Vision and Fusion Laboratory
Institute for Anthropomatics
Karlsruhe Institute of Technology (KIT), Germany
mathias.anneken@kit.edu

Technical Report IES-2018-09

Abstract

This report focuses on extending the object-oriented world model by a behaviour model for its representatives. The world model in general is used as a foundation for fusing multiple sensor sources into one coherent picture. It should enable other services to access the stored information for further processing, e.g. for recognizing suspicious situations in surveillance tasks. While the base model is able to capture the real world entities by translating them into representatives while incorporating background-knowledge in form of concepts, it is not able to predict the behaviour of these representatives. Here, a concept based on intelligent rational agents is introduced.

1 Introduction

Given the humongous amount of heterogeneous data generated by the multitude of sensor sources (e.g. RADAR, cameras, ...), as well as the complex and demanding task itself, due to its time pressure, inconsistencies, imperfect and in general quite uncertain information, surveillance tasks, e.g. in the maritime domain, are quite challenging for human operators. Therefore automatic system are created to assist and support the operators during decision making processes.

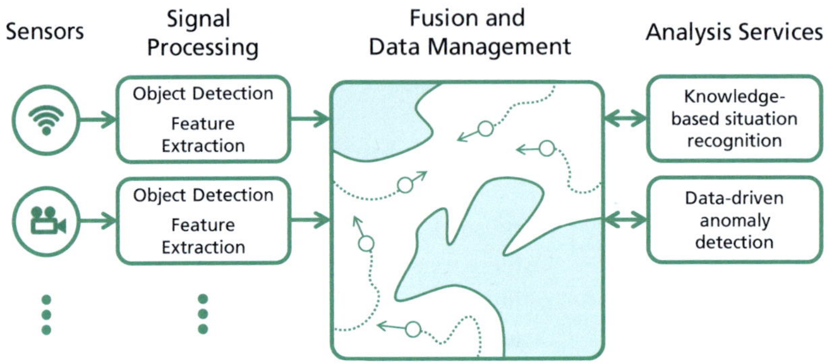

Figure 1.1: General structure for situation analysis task in surveillance applications.

Such an automatic system shall infer the existence of situations $\mathcal{S}$ by observing all entities $\mathcal{E}$ in the real world while incorporating the available background knowledge for the given application domain. The inference of the existence of a situation is called situation analysis.

The incoming data from the sensor systems will be processed and object are detected and their features are extracted. This information is the base for different situation analysis algorithms, either knowledge-based or data-driven. Figure 1.1 gives an overview of the whole task: Sensors will capture the entities translate them to objects in the fusion and data management system, which will be used as foundation for the analysis services. In order to utilize this information a model for representing it is needed. Here, the Object-Oriented World Model (OOWM) is used.

2 Object-Oriented World Model

The OOWM was first introduced by Gheta et al. in [GHB08]. It is the foundation for reasoning of autonomous systems [BGB$^+$10, GHBB10, GBB$^+$10, BKFB12, Bel15]. This approach has a fixed background knowledge. In [Kuw10, Kuw12a, Kuw12b] first steps towards an adaptive open-world modelling are given. This was further described and elaborated in [KB13a, KS13, KB13b, KB14, KGHB15, KB16]. For surveillance tasks, it is used in [KFEPB12, Fis16].

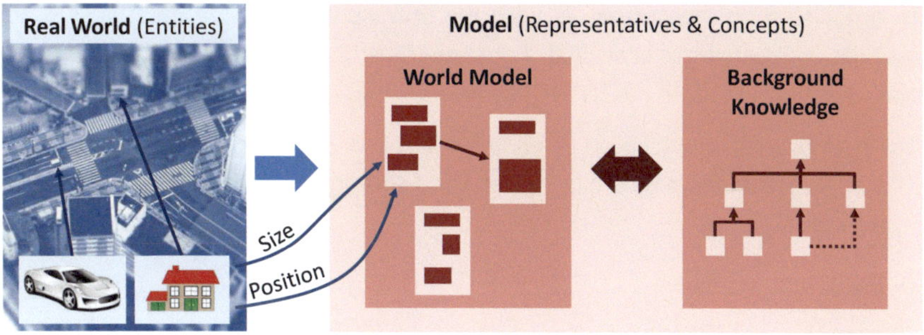

Figure 2.1: Schematic structure of the OOWM.

Here, the formalization of the OOWM stated by Kuwertz and Beyerer in [KB16] is adopted.

The OOWM is a computational representation of the real world. Its main components are shown in Figure 2.1. It is generated by using the information acquired by sensor observations. This model is then considered a consistent representation of the current state. It can act as the foundation of higher level data fusion services in order to assess a situation at hand, support the decision making process, and improving thus the situational awareness. In order to improve the model, background knowledge in form of conceptual models relevant for the application domain are incorporated.

The model builds representatives for all entities $\mathcal{E}$ in the real world, which are observed by the available sensors (and relevant for the application domain).

Definition 3 (Representative). *A representative $R \in \mathcal{R}$ is given by the set of attributes $\mathcal{A}_R = \{A_1, \ldots, A_n\}, n \in \mathbb{N}$.*

Definition 4 (Attribute). *An attribute A_i is represented by the probability distribution $p_{A_i}(a)$ (Degree of Belief (DoB) in attribute values). This distribution $p_{A_i}(a)$ is either discrete or continuous.*

The representative R are given by the joint probability distribution

$$p(R) = p(\mathcal{A}_R) = \prod_{i=1,\ldots,n} p_{A_i}(a) \; .$$

In order to map the entities $\mathcal{E}$ with the corresponding representatives $\mathcal{R}$, an association mechanism is needed. For further readings into this topic, relate to the work by Baum et al. in [BGB$^+$10].

The background knowledge is given in form of concepts $\mathcal{C}$. These concepts consist of a set of attributes which can be used as a prototype for representatives in the world model.

Definition 5 (Concept). *A concept $C \in \mathcal{C}$ s given by the set of attributes $\mathcal{A}_C = \{A_1, \ldots, A_m\}, m \in \mathbb{N}$. A concept C may be represented by the joint probability distribution $p(C) = p(\mathcal{A}_C) = \prod_{i=1,\ldots,m} p_{A_i}(a)$.*

Definition 6 (The Association probability of representative R to concept C).

$$p(C \mid R) = \frac{1}{z} \cdot p(C) \cdot \prod_{A_i \in \mathcal{A}_R} \left(\int_{\mathbb{R}} p_{A_i}(a) \cdot p_{A_c}(a) \, \mathrm{d}a \right)$$

with A_c as corresponding attribute of the concept C for the attribute A_i of R and z as normalization parameter.

3 Situation

The formalization of a Situation is in line with [Fis16]. According to Ye et al. [YDM12],

> "A situation is defined as an external semantic interpretation of sensor data. Interpretation means that situations assign meanings to sensor data. External means that the interpretation is from the perspective of applications, rather than from sensors. Semantic means that the interpretation assigns meaning on sensor data based on structures and relationships within the same type of sensor data and between different types of sensor data."

Following the definitions in section 2, the entities $\mathcal{E}$ in the real world are described in the OOWM as representatives $\mathcal{R}$. As a situation S is not necessarily depending on all representatives, the subset of relevant ones are given by $\mathcal{R}^r \subseteq \mathcal{R}$.

Definition 7 (State space of a situation).

$$\Omega_S := \bigtimes_{R \in \mathcal{R}^r} R \times \mathbb{T} = \bigtimes_{R \in \mathcal{R}^r} \bigtimes_{A_i \in \mathcal{A}_R} A_i \times \mathbb{T}$$

$\mathbb{T}$ represents the time domain. A point in time $t \in \mathbb{T}$ can either be continuous $\mathbb{T} = \mathbb{R}_0^+$ or discrete $\mathbb{T} = \mathbb{N}$.

Definition 8 (Situation at a point in time). *A situation S_t is defined for the time t as the mapping*

$$S_t \colon \Omega_S \to \{0, 1\} \ .$$

Where $S_t = 0$ or $\bar{S}_t$ denotes, that a situation does not exists, and $S_t = 1$ or S_t that the situation exists.

For the time t an element of the state space is given by $\omega_t \in \Omega_S$. A trajectory through the state space is then defined for a time interval $d = \{t_1, t_2, \ldots, t_k\}$ by the elements $\omega_d = (\omega_{t_1}, \omega_{t_2}, \ldots, \omega_{t_k})$.

Definition 9 (Situation over a time interval). *A situation S_d given the time interval d is defined as*

$$S_d \colon \bigtimes_{i=1}^{k} \Omega_S \to \{0, 1\} \ .$$

The existence of a situation at time t (analogously for time interval d) can be described by probabilistic means. Hence, the situation S_t can be interpreted as a binary random variable:

- Σ_S is a sigma-algebra on Ω_S, thus a subset of the power set of Ω_S.
- p is a probability measure on (Ω_S, Σ_S).

Definition 10 (Existence of a situation). *(Ω_S, Σ_S, P) is a probability space and p a distribution for S_t with the existence probability given by*

$$p(S_t = s), \text{ with } s \in \{0, 1\} \ .$$

So far, the existence of a situation can be inferred by using the trajectory ω_d. But ω_d depends on the behaviour of the entities $\mathcal{E}$ and their interactions with each other. Integrating the specific behaviour of each entity might have a huge impact on the situation analysis, as it might give explanations for valid and righteous behaviour even though at first glance it seems to be just erratic. This arises the question about "how to model the behaviour?".

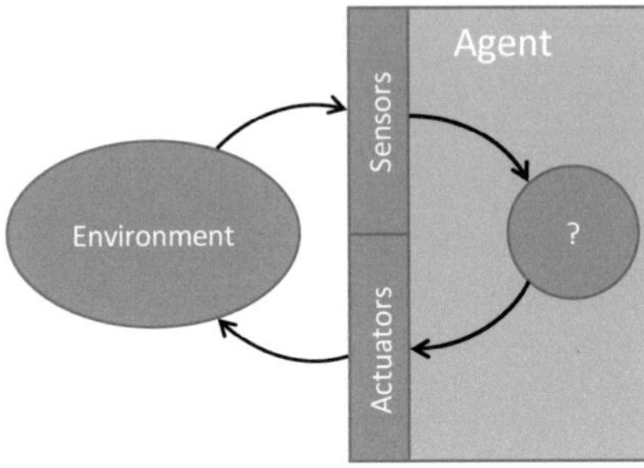

Figure 4.1: Intelligent Agent. [RN95]

4 Expending the OOWM with Agents

Not all entities will have a dedicated behaviour relying on a reasoning process, e.g. inanimate entities like a cup. For all others, the assumption of an agent model seems to be a fitting choice, as Russell and Norvig state in [RN95]:

> "An agent is anything that can be viewed as perceiving its environment through sensors and acting upon that environment through effectors."

As seen in Figure 4.1, such an agent is able to perceive the environment using its sensors, resulting in a subset of representatives in the OOWM $\mathcal{R}^p \subseteq \mathcal{R}$. Further the agent can carry out actions $\mathcal{B}$ with its actuators, which will effect the environment. These actions will influence the attributes of the entities in the real world.

An intelligent agent will use some reasoning process to decide on the action to take. Thus results the characterization for an ideal rational agent by Russell and Norvig [RN95] as follows:

> "For each possible percept sequence, an ideal rational agent should do whatever action is expected to maximize its performance measure, on the basis of evidence provided by the percept sequence and whatever built-in knowledge the agent has."

This can be adapted to the formalization for situations as follows: For the observation made by the entity E, the resulting state space is given by

$$\Omega_E := \bigtimes_{R \in \mathcal{R}^r} (R, \mathcal{C}_R^r) \times \mathbb{T}$$

and $\mathcal{R}^r \subseteq \mathcal{R}^p$ is the set of all observed representatives, which are relevant for a decision. Further, $\mathcal{C}_R^r$ denotes all relevant concepts for the representative R.

The behaviour H of an agent over a time interval $d = (t_1, \ldots, t_k)$ is the mapping of the state space Ω_E to an action $B \in \mathcal{B}$:

$$H\colon \bigtimes_{i=1}^{k} \Omega_E \to B$$

The set of possible mapping is denoted with $\mathcal{H}$.

This implies, that some of the representatives in the OOWM will behave like a rational agent. Thus, the background knowledge needs to be extended by the set of behaviour models:

Definition 11 (Behaviour in the OOWM)**.** *The set of possible behaviour mappings $\mathcal{H}$ is part of the background knowledge. A representative may follow a specific behaviour $H \in \mathcal{H}$ based on the given concept C.*

Definition 12 (Association between representative and behaviour)**.** *The association between the behaviour H and a representative R is given by*

$$P(H \mid C),\ \forall H \in \mathcal{H}, \forall C \in \mathcal{C}, \text{with } P(C \mid R) > 0\ .$$

These definitions allow each representative to follow a behaviour based on its associated concepts. For the next step, the behaviour needs to be filled with a model for actually choosing an appropriate action given all the available information.

5 Behaviour model

Following Russell and Norvig [RN95], there are multiple models for an agent to make a decision. One of these is a utility-based agent as shown in Figure 5.1. This agent will perceive its environment and build a representation of the world. It is able to infer the effects of its own actions on the environment. A utility function is then used to decide on the one action which will maximize the gain for the agent. This action will be carried out by its effectors.

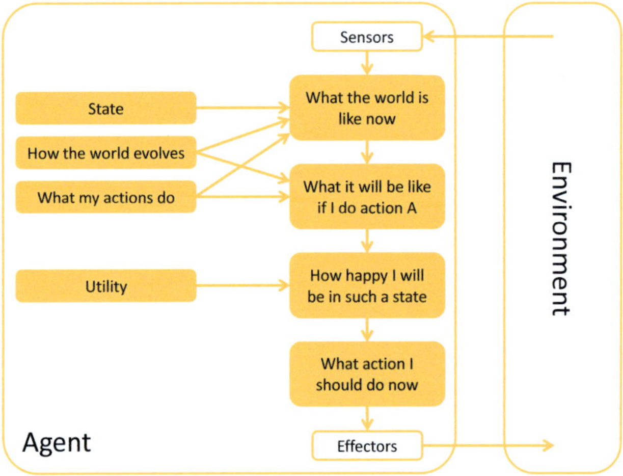

Figure 5.1: Utility-based agent. [RN95]

Another concept for an agent is given by Rao and Georgeff in [RG95]. It is called an BDI agent:

- Beliefs: Observed knowledge of the agent about himself and the world.
- Desires: States that solve a problem.
- Intentions: Possible plans or strategies for achieving the objectives.

An addition to this model is given by Broersen et al. in [BDH$^+$01]. The idea is to include obligations, which will hold values, norms and rules applicable to all agents.

While this models define a general concept about how to decide on an action, it is still unclear, how the goals are defined and how exactly decisions are made. A famous example of this issue is given by Lewis Caroll in his novel Alice's Adventures in Wonderland:

> "Alice: *Would you tell me, please, which way I ought to go from here?*
> The Cheshire Cat: *That depends a good deal on where you want to get to.*
> Alice: *I don't much care where.*
> The Cheshire Cat: *Then it doesn't much matter which way you go.*
> Alice: ... *So long as I get somewhere.*
> The Cheshire Cat: *Oh, you're sure to do that, if only you walk long enough.*"

Therefore, without a valid objective in mind, it is quite impossible to decide on the right action, or any action would be ok.

The decision theory is the study of analysing the choices made by agents. It splits into two branches: normative and descriptive decision theory.

> "The distinction between normative and descriptive decision theories is, in principle, very simple. A normative decision theory is a theory about how decisions should be made, and a descriptive theory is a theory about how decisions are actually made." [Han94]

A major drawback of decision theory is, that it is only concerned with the choices made by a singular agent. Closely related is the field of game theory. In game theory, the choices of agents, which actions will interfere with each other, are analysed.

Thus, "[g]ame theory can be defined as the study of mathematical models of conflict and cooperation between intelligent rational decision-makers" [Mye07]. The decision making is described in form of games:

Definition 13 (Game)**.** *A (non-cooperative) game Γ consists of a set of players $\mathcal{N}$, a set of strategies $\mathcal{B}$ and the utility function u:*

$$\Gamma = (\mathcal{N}, \mathcal{B}, u)$$

Definition 14 (Players)**.** *Each representative $R \in \mathcal{R}$ with a behaviour H can be interpreted as a player in a game Γ. The set of players is given by*

$$\mathcal{N} = \{1, \ldots, n\} \, .$$

Definition 15 (Strategies). *A strategy B of a player $i \in \mathcal{N}$ corresponds to an action $\mathcal{B}_i$ each representative R_i can choose of. Thus, the set of all strategies is given by*

$$\mathcal{B} = \bigtimes_{i=1}^{n} \mathcal{B}_i \ .$$

Definition 16 (Utility function). *A utility is mapped to all players for each strategy combination:*

$$u \colon \mathcal{B} \to \mathbb{R}^n \ .$$

There are solution concepts for this kind of games like the Nash equilibrium [Nas51]. Such a game is a model for a non-cooperative situation, that means, that the agents will try to maximize their own utility, but they will not try to increase the gain for each other. Going back to the surveillance task, this often does not apply, because the agents might want to work together to increase the overall utility. To counter this challenge, cooperative games were designed, e.g. a bargaining game:

Definition 17 (Bargaining game). *An extension of a game Γ by a conflict point c is called a (cooperative) bargaining game*

$$\Gamma_B = (\mathcal{N}, P, c) \ ,$$

whereas P denotes the payoff space with all the feasible utility results

$$P = \{u(B) \mid B \in \mathcal{B}\} \ ,$$

and the conflict point $c \in P$ is the utility gained by the players, if they do not agree on a solution.

This kind of game will allow solution concepts like the Nash bargaining solution [Nas53] to follow specific axioms, which define a fair and reasonable outcome for all players in a bargaining situation.

Following the OOWM's concepts, the behaviour of each agent should be depending on their type. One game to follow this notion, is a Bayesian game [Har68], in which each player will be assigned a specific type influencing the utility. The type will be chosen by nature (modeled as a special player).

Definition 18 (Bayesian game). *A game with incomplete information extended by types for the players is given by*

$$\Gamma_{\mathit{Bayesian}} = (\mathcal{N}, (\mathcal{T}_i, \mathcal{B}_i, u_i, p_i)_{i\in\mathcal{N}}) .$$

The nature will assign randomly the types for the players. The players only know their own type.

The type $\mathcal{T}$ of a player will define its preferences (utility) and strategies. Before any player can act, the nature will choose the type $T_i \in \mathcal{T}_i$ for each player $i \in \mathcal{N}$. Compared to the general game, the utility function needs to be adjusted. It has to assign a value not only to the combinations of strategies, but also for the types:

$$u\colon \mathcal{B} \times \mathcal{T} \to \mathbb{R}^n .$$

The belief p_i of player $i \in \mathcal{N}$ is a probability distribution for the types.

Translating a Bayesian game to the OOWM will result in the following mapping:

- Players are representatives: $\mathcal{N} \to \mathcal{R}$
- Types are concepts: $\mathcal{T} \to$ concepts $\mathcal{C}$
- Beliefs in the types are probability distribution over the assigned concept for each representative: $p_i \to p(C \mid R)$ for $R \in \mathcal{R}^p$

For solving a game, many solution concepts were introduced over the course of time. For non-cooperative games this includes: rationalizability and iterated dominance, Nash equilibrium, Bayesian Nash equilibrium. The Nash equilibrium was for example used by Anneken in [Ann16] as a solution concept to estimate the behaviour of ships. Some solution concepts for cooperative games are the core, Nash bargaining solution and Kalai-Smorodinski bargaining solution. The Nash bargaining solution was used by Anneken et al. in [AFB17] to estimate the behaviour for multiple cooperating vessels in the maritime domain.

6 Situation analysis

The main idea here is to use the extended OOWM for situation analysis in surveillance tasks. Thus $\mathcal{R}$ are all representatives of the entities $\mathcal{E}$ of the real world.

There is an observer responsible for the surveillance task. This observer is an entity itself: $E_O \in \mathcal{E}$. The corresponding representative is given by $R_O \in \mathcal{R}$. Each observer has its own background knowledge, which includes the concepts $\mathcal{C}_O$ and behaviour models $\mathcal{H}_O$. The observer R_O can perceive a subset of the entities which results in the following set of representatives $\mathcal{R}_O^p \subseteq \mathcal{R}$.

Each of the observed representatives $R \in \mathcal{R}_O^p$ will base its action $B_R \in \mathcal{B}_R$ on other representatives perceived by it $\mathcal{R}_R^p \subseteq \mathcal{R}$, the concepts $\mathcal{C}_R$ and the behaviour model $\mathcal{H}_R$.

The observer will base his anticipations regarding the behaviour of the representatives $\mathcal{R}_O^p$ on his background knowledge $\mathcal{H}_O$ and on each of the perceived representatives. The entities in the real world will base their behaviour H on their own observations. In case, that the observer is able to perceive the same relevant part of the world as the representative, the expected behaviour and the actual behaviour should be the same. It will deviate, if the concepts $\mathcal{C}$, the behaviours $\mathcal{H}$, or the observed representative $\mathcal{R}_O^p$ do not match.

By comparing the predicted behaviour with the actual, it is possible to make a statement about the possibility $p(H_O \mid H_R)$. This has been done e.g. in [AFB16a, AFB16b] by geometric comparisons of movement patterns using the Hausdorff metric or dynamic time warping. Another approach was shown in [Ann16, AFB17], where a utility function was developed, which was in turn used to participate a behaviour. The utility by the actual behaviour is than compared with the one from the estimated strategy.

The information gained about the probability $p(H_O \mid H_R)$ can then be used for the mapping between the entities and the situation $S \in \mathcal{S}$ at hand: An entity, which behaviour deviates, can be considered an anomaly, while at the same time the probability for an expected illegal action can be estimated by modelling it as possible behaviour.

7 Conclusion and Future Work

A concept for integrating a behaviour model into the OOWM was introduced. This model is based on a game theoretic approach. While the OOWM is already incorporating methods for associating real world entities with the computational representatives based on background-knowledge in form of concepts, it is not able to predict behaviour or give inside into the decision process of entities. The addition of utility based intelligent agents, which will make a decision based on the results of a Bayesian game, will address this shortcomings. This will allow a surveillance system to support an operator with even more inside.

Additional to the introduced extension, the next steps will include further research into a prototype, the estimation and prediction of actions, and based on this the detection of anomalies or suspicious behaviour. One important step will be the design of the utility function.

Bibliography

[AFB16a] Mathias Anneken, Yvonne Fischer, and Jürgen Beyerer. Anomaly detection using b-spline control points as feature space in annotated trajectory data from the maritime domain. In *Proceedings of the 8th International Conference on Agents and Artificial Intelligence*, volume 2, pages 250–257, 2016.

[AFB16b] Mathias Anneken, Yvonne Fischer, and Jürgen Beyerer. Detection of conspicuous behavior in street traffic by using b-splines as feature vector. In *Proceedings of the 11th Security Research Conference (Future Security)*, pages 325–331. Fraunhofer Verlag, 2016.

[AFB17] Mathias Anneken, Yvonne Fischer, and Jürgen Beyerer. A multi-agent approach to model and analyze the behavior of vessels in the maritime domain. In *Proceedings of the 9th International Conference on Agents and Artificial Intelligence - Volume 1: ICAART*, pages 200–207, 2017.

[Ann16] Mathias Anneken. Anomaly detection using the nash equilibirum in a multi-agent system. In *Joint Workshop of Fraunhofer IOSB and Institute for Anthropomatics, Vision and Fusion Laboratory 2016*, pages 325–331. Fraunhofer Verlag, 2016.

[BDH+01] Jan Broersen, Mehdi Dastani, Joris Hulstijn, Zisheng Huang, and Leendert van der Torre. The BOID Architecture - Conflicts Between Beliefs, Obligations, Intentions and Desires. In *In Proceedings of the Fifth International Conference on Autonomous Agents*, pages 9–16. ACM Press, 2001.

[Bel15] Andrey Belkin. *World Modeling for Intelligent Autonomous Systems*. PhD thesis, Institut für Anthropomatik und Robotik (IAR) Fakultät für Informatik (INFORMATIK), 2015.

[BGB+10] Marcus Baum, Ioana Gheta, Andrey Belkin, Jürgen Beyerer, and Uwe D. Hanebeck. Data association in a world model for autonomous systems.

In *2010 IEEE Conference on Multisensor Fusion and Integration*, pages 187–192, Sept 2010.

[BKFB12] Andrey Belkin, Achim Kuwertz, Yvonne Fischer, and Jürgen Beyerer. World modeling for autonomous systems. In Christos Kalloniatis, editor, *Innovative Information Systems Modelling Techniques*. InTech - Open Access Publisher, May 2012.

[Fis16] Yvonne Fischer. *Wissensbasierte probabilistische Modellierung für die Situationsanalyse am Beispiel der maritimen Überwachung*. PhD thesis, Karlsruhe Institute of Technology, 2016.

[GBB⁺10] Ioana Gheta, Marcus Baum, Andrey Belkin, Jürgen Beyerer, and Uwe D. Hanebeck. Three pillar information management system for modeling the environment of autonomous systems. In *Proceedings of IEEE Conference on Virtual Environments, Human-Computer Interfaces and Measurement Systems*, pages 12–17, Taranto, September 2010.

[GHB08] Ioana Gheta, Michael Heizmann, and Jürgen Beyerer. Object oriented environment model for autonomous systems. In Henrik Boström, Ronnie Johansson, and Joeri van Laere, editors, *Proceedings of the second Skövde Workshop on Information Fusion Topics*, pages 9–12. Skövde Studies in Informatics, November 2008.

[GHBB10] Ioana Gheta, Michael Heizmann, Andrey Belkin, and Jürgen Beyerer. World modeling for autonomous systems. In Rüdiger Dillmann, Jürgen Beyerer, Uwe D. Hanebeck, and Tanja Schultz, editors, *KI 2010: Advances in Artificial Intelligence*, volume 6359 of *Lecture Notes in Artificial Intelligence*, pages 176–183, Karlsruhe, September 2010. Springer.

[Han94] Sven Ove Hansson. Decision theory: A brief introduction. 1994.

[Har68] John C. Harsanyi. Games with incomplete information played by "bayesian" players, i-iii. part ii. bayesian equilibrium points. *Management Science*, 14(5):320–334, 1968.

[KB13a] Achim Kuwertz and Jürgen Beyerer. Knowledge model quantitative evaluation for adaptive world modeling. In *Proceedings of the IEEE Conference on Cognitive Methods in Situation Awareness and Decision Support (CogSIMA 2013), 2013*, San Diego, USA, February 2013.

[KB13b] Achim Kuwertz and Jürgen Beyerer. Quantitative measures for adaptive object-oriented world modeling. In *Proceedings of 4th Workshop on Dynamics of Knowledge and Belief at the 36th Annual German Conference on Artificial Intelligence (KI-2013)*, pages 89–104, Koblenz, September 2013. FernUniversität in Hagen, Hagen.

[KB14] Achim Kuwertz and Jürgen Beyerer. Dealing with poorly mapped entities in adaptive object-oriented world modeling. In *Proceedings of the IEEE International Inter-Disciplinary Conference on Cognitive Methods in Situation Awareness and Decision Support (CogSIMA) 2014*, San Antonio, USA, March 2014.

[KB16] Achim Kuwertz and Jürgen Beyerer. Extending adaptive world modeling by identifying and handling insufficient knowledge models. *Journal of Applied Logic*, 19:102 – 127, 2016. SI:Dynamics of Knowledge and Belief.

[KFEPB12] Achim Kuwertz, Yvonne Fischer, Barbara Essendorfer, and Elisabeth Peinsipp-Byma. Using context knowledge for maritime situation assessment. In *Proceedings of 3rd International Conference on WaterSide Security*, Singapore, May 2012.

[KGHB15] Achim Kuwertz, Cornelius Goldbeck, Ronny Hug, and Jürgen Beyerer. Towards web-based semantic knowledge completion for adaptive world modeling in cognitive systems. In *2015 17th UKSim-AMSS International Conference on Modelling and Simulation (UKSim)*, pages 165–170, March 2015.

[KS13] Achim Kuwertz and Gerd Schneider. Ontology-based meta model in object-oriented world modeling for interoperable information access. In *Proceedings of the Eighth International Conference on Systems (ICONS 2013)*, Seville, Spain, January 2013.

[Kuw10] Achim Kuwertz. On adaptive open-world modeling based on information fusion and inductive inference. Technical Report IES-2010-16, Karlsruher Institut für Technologie, 2010.

[Kuw12a] Achim Kuwertz. Extending object-oriented world modeling for adaptive open-world modeling. Technical Report IES-2012-06, Karlsruher Institut für Technologie, 2012.

[Kuw12b] Achim Kuwertz. Towards adaptive open-world modeling. Technical Report IES-2011-10, Karlsruher Institut für Technologie, 2012.

[Mye07] Roger B. Myerson. *Game theory: analysis of conflict*. Harvard Univ. Press, 2007.

[Nas51] John Nash. Non-cooperative games. *Annals of mathematics*, pages 286–295, 1951.

[Nas53] John Nash. Two-person cooperative games. *Econometrica: Journal of the Econometric Society*, pages 128–140, 1953.

[RG95] Anand S. Rao and Michael P. Georgeff. BDI Agents: From Theory to Practice. In *In Proceedings of the First International Conference on Multi-agent Systems*, pages 312–319, 1995.

[RN95] Stuart Russell and Peter Norvig. *Artificial Intelligence: A Modern Approach*. Prentice Hall, 1995.

[YDM12] Juan Ye, Simon Dobson, and Susan McKeever. Situation identification techniques in pervasive computing: A review. *Pervasive and Mobile Computing*, 8(1):36–66, 2012.

Karlsruher Schriftenreihe zur Anthropomatik (ISSN 1863-6489)

Herausgeber: Prof. Dr.-Ing. habil. Jürgen Beyerer

Band 1 Jürgen Geisler
Leistung des Menschen am Bildschirmarbeitsplatz. 2006
ISBN 3-86644-070-7

Band 2 Elisabeth Peinsipp-Byma
Leistungserhöhung durch Assistenz in interaktiven Systemen zur Szenenanalyse. 2007
ISBN 978-3-86644-149-1

Band 3 Jürgen Geisler, Jürgen Beyerer (Hrsg.)
Mensch-Maschine-Systeme. 2010
ISBN 978-3-86644-457-7

Band 4 Jürgen Beyerer, Marco Huber (Hrsg.)
Proceedings of the 2009 Joint Workshop of Fraunhofer IOSB and Institute for Anthropomatics, Vision and Fusion Laboratory. 2010
ISBN 978-3-86644-469-0

Band 5 Thomas Usländer
Service-oriented design of environmental information systems. 2010
ISBN 978-3-86644-499-7

Band 6 Giulio Milighetti
Multisensorielle diskret-kontinuierliche Überwachung und Regelung humanoider Roboter. 2010
ISBN 978-3-86644-568-0

Band 7 Jürgen Beyerer, Marco Huber (Hrsg.)
Proceedings of the 2010 Joint Workshop of Fraunhofer IOSB and Institute for Anthropomatics, Vision and Fusion Laboratory. 2011
ISBN 978-3-86644-609-0

Band 8 Eduardo Monari
Dynamische Sensorselektion zur auftragsorientierten Objektverfolgung in Kameranetzwerken. 2011
ISBN 978-3-86644-729-5

Die Bände sind unter www.ksp.kit.edu als PDF frei verfügbar oder als Druckausgabe bestellbar.

Band 9 Thomas Bader
Multimodale Interaktion in Multi-Display-Umgebungen. 2011
ISBN 3-86644-760-8

Band 10 Christian Frese
Planung kooperativer Fahrmanöver für kognitive Automobile. 2012
ISBN 978-3-86644-798-1

Band 11 Jürgen Beyerer, Alexey Pak (Hrsg.)
Proceedings of the 2011 Joint Workshop of Fraunhofer IOSB and Institute for Anthropomatics, Vision and Fusion Laboratory. 2012
ISBN 978-3-86644-855-1

Band 12 Miriam Schleipen
Adaptivität und Interoperabilität von Manufacturing Execution Systemen (MES). 2013
ISBN 978-3-86644-955-8

Band 13 Jürgen Beyerer, Alexey Pak (Hrsg.)
Proceedings of the 2012 Joint Workshop of Fraunhofer IOSB and Institute for Anthropomatics, Vision and Fusion Laboratory. 2013
ISBN 978-3-86644-988-6

Band 14 Hauke-Hendrik Vagts
Privatheit und Datenschutz in der intelligenten Überwachung: Ein datenschutzgewährendes System, entworfen nach dem „Privacy by Design“ Prinzip. 2013
ISBN 978-3-7315-0041-4

Band 15 Christian Kühnert
Data-driven Methods for Fault Localization in Process Technology. 2013
ISBN 978-3-7315-0098-8

Band 16 Alexander Bauer
Probabilistische Szenenmodelle für die Luftbildauswertung. 2014
ISBN 978-3-7315-0167-1

Band 17 Jürgen Beyerer, Alexey Pak (Hrsg.)
Proceedings of the 2013 Joint Workshop of Fraunhofer IOSB and Institute for Anthropomatics, Vision and Fusion Laboratory. 2014
ISBN 978-3-7315-0212-8

Band 18 Michael Teutsch
Moving Object Detection and Segmentation for Remote Aerial Video Surveillance. 2015
ISBN 978-3-7315-0320-0

Band 19 Marco Huber
Nonlinear Gaussian Filtering: Theory, Algorithms, and Applications. 2015
ISBN 978-3-7315-0338-5

Band 20 Jürgen Beyerer, Alexey Pak (Hrsg.)
Proceedings of the 2014 Joint Workshop of Fraunhofer IOSB and Institute for Anthropomatics, Vision and Fusion Laboratory. 2014
ISBN 978-3-7315-0401-6

Band 21 Todor Dimitrov
Permanente Optimierung dynamischer Probleme der Fertigungssteuerung unter Einbeziehung von Benutzerinteraktionen. 2015
ISBN 978-3-7315-0426-9

Band 22 Benjamin Kühn
Interessengetriebene audiovisuelle Szenenexploration. 2016
ISBN 978-3-7315-0457-3

Band 23 Yvonne Fischer
Wissensbasierte probabilistische Modellierung für die Situationsanalyse am Beispiel der maritimen Überwachung. 2016
ISBN 978-3-7315-0460-3

Band 24 Jürgen Beyerer, Alexey Pak (Hrsg.)
Proceedings of the 2015 Joint Workshop of Fraunhofer IOSB and Institute for Anthropomatics, Vision and Fusion Laboratory. 2016
ISBN 978-3-7315-0519-8

Band 25 Pascal Birnstill
Privacy-Respecting Smart Video Surveillance Based on Usage Control Enforcement. 2016
ISBN 978-3-7315-0538-9

Band 26 Philipp Woock
Umgebungskartenschätzung aus Sidescan-Sonardaten für ein autonomes Unterwasserfahrzeug. 2016
ISBN 978-3-7315-0541-9

Band 27 Janko Petereit
Adaptive State × Time Lattices: A Contribution to Mobile Robot Motion Planning in Unstructured Dynamic Environments. 2017
ISBN 978-3-7315-0580-8

Band 28 Erik Ludwig Krempel
Steigerung der Akzeptanz von intelligenter Videoüberwachung in öffentlichen Räumen. 2017
ISBN 978-3-7315-0598-3

Band 29 Jürgen Moßgraber
Ein Rahmenwerk für die Architektur von Frühwarnsystemen. 2017
ISBN 978-3-7315-0638-6

Band 30 Andrey Belkin
World Modeling for Intelligent Autonomous Systems. 2017
ISBN 978-3-7315-0641-6

Band 31 Chettapong Janya-Anurak
Framework for Analysis and Identification of Nonlinear Distributed Parameter Systems using Bayesian Uncertainty Quantification based on Generalized Polynomial Chaos. 2017
ISBN 978-3-7315-0642-3

Band 32 David Münch
Begriffliche Situationsanalyse aus Videodaten bei unvollständiger und fehlerhafter Information. 2017
ISBN 978-3-7315-0644-7

Band 33 Jürgen Beyerer, Alexey Pak (Eds.)
Proceedings of the 2016 Joint Workshop of Fraunhofer IOSB and Institute for Anthropomatics, Vision and Fusion Laboratory. 2017
ISBN 978-3-7315-0678-2

Band 34 Jürgen Beyerer, Alexey Pak and Miro Taphanel (Eds.)
Proceedings of the 2017 Joint Workshop of Fraunhofer IOSB and Institute for Anthropomatics, Vision and Fusion Laboratory. 2018
ISBN 978-3-7315-0779-6

Band 35 Michael Grinberg
Feature-Based Probabilistic Data Association for Video-Based Multi-Object Tracking. 2018
ISBN 978-3-7315-0781-9

Band 36 Christian Herrmann
Video-to-Video Face Recognition for Low-Quality Surveillance Data. 2018
ISBN 978-3-7315-0799-4

Band 37 Chengchao Qu
Facial Texture Super-Resolution by Fitting 3D Face Models. 2018
ISBN 978-3-7315-0828-1

Band 38 Miriam Ruf
Geometrie und Topologie von Trajektorienoptimierung für vollautomatisches Fahren. 2018
ISBN 978-3-7315-0832-8

Band 39 Angelika Zube
Bewegungsregelung mobiler Manipulatoren für die Mensch-Roboter-Interaktion mittels kartesischer modellprädiktiver Regelung. 2018
ISBN 978-3-7315-0855-7

Band 40 Jürgen Beyerer and Miro Taphanel (Eds.)
Proceedings of the 2018 Joint Workshop of Fraunhofer IOSB and Institute for Anthropomatics, Vision and Fusion Laboratory. 2019
ISBN 978-3-7315-0936-3

Die Bände sind unter www.ksp.kit.edu als PDF frei verfügbar oder als Druckausgabe bestellbar.